Nancy Ward
CHEROKEE CHIEFTAINESS
—*Her cry was all for peace*—

Dragging Canoe
CHEROKEE-CHICKAMAUGA WAR CHIEF
—*We are not yet conquered*—

Pat Alderman

Second Edition
(INDEX ADDED)

Cover Art by Timothy N. Tate

JOHNSON CITY, TENNESSEE

ACKNOWLEDGMENTS

The writer owes many thanks to many people who have contributed time, materials, and professional assistance toward preparing the script, illustrations, and photographs for this publication.

Special thanks go to Judy Blevins for editing script and helpful advice, and to JoLinda Lewis for typesetting and paste-up. Without the aid of these two capable associates this publication would have been doubtful. Thanks to Edyth Price for many inside sketches; Dr. Duane H. King for materials and pictures; Cherokee Historical Association for use of Oconaluftee Village Scenes; Bernie Andrews and Kenneth Ferguson for illustrations used from *The Overmountain Men* publication; Mary Hardin McCown for materials; Harry D. Switzer for photos of Nancy Ward grave and markers, Benton, Tennessee; Jim Turner and Mrs. Mac Satterwhite for copy reading; Roy Lilliard for material and pictures; Earl Walker for color transparencies; Sandra Harrison, Librarian at Qualla Boundary Public Library, Cherokee, North Carolina, and Maxine Jones, Librarian at Unicoi County Library, Erwin, Tennessee, as well as Muskogee Public Library, Muskogee, Oklahoma, for securing materials; Sandra Roberts for typing and copy assistance; and to Duke Barr, Carolyn Miller, Vernon Sims, Hal Spoden, Jack Lane, Archer Blevins, Danny Lewis, and many others.

(THIS COPY INCLUDED IN FIRST EDITION)

DOCUMENTARY FILM OF NANCY WARD-DRAGGING CANOE BOOK

WSJK-TV Channel 2, East Tennessee State University Studios, Johnson City, Tennessee, is preparing a documentary film of the Nancy Ward-Dragging Canoe scripts written by Pat Alderman. Under the guidance of Producer/Director Richard W. Hall, this sixty-minute film will be made available to any PBS station in the United States.

Edyth Price is art contributor and color advisor for film material; and Polly King is preparing needed slides. Other contributions and contributors include: Harry D. Switzer, scenes of Polk County, Tennessee area, last home and burial place of Nancy Ward; New York Public Library, color copies of White-de Bry paintings of southeastern Indian culture of 1580-1590, secured by Elaine Guinn; Cherokee Historical Association, Cherokee, North Carolina, scenes from re-created Indian Village *Oconaluftee* of two hundred years ago; Walter Williams, President of Great American Publishing Co., Chattanooga, Tennessee, for use of *The Little Tennessee River Valley* by Chester Martin; *Fort Loudoun* and *Chota* by Louis Spitzer, from the private collection of Fidelity Federal Savings, Knoxville, Tennessee; Charles Pugh, scenes from restored Cherokee capital (New Echota) Calhoun, Georgia; Tom and Alma Gray, scenes from re-created Fort Watauga, Elizabethton, Tennessee; E.C. Wilson, White's Fort, Knoxville, Tennessee; illustrations by Bernie Andrews, from Alderman's *The Overmountain Men* and (two) from Mary U. Rothrock's *This Is Tennessee;* other illustrations, Kenneth Ferguson and Robert Panell; also Jan Barr, Carol Morrell, Roy Lillard, Gene Price, Vernon Sims, Tennessee State Museum; and Tennessee Department of Conservation. Special thanks go to Elizabethton (Tennessee) High School Art Department teacher Robert Pannell and students Randy Johnson, Bart Cable, Dale Johnson, Ted Sammons, William Trammell, Danney Wilson, Robert Campbell, Nathaniel Machey, Darrell Woods, Joseph Nanney, John Gouge, Barbara McGinty, Robert Michael, Gwen O'Hare, and Ben Watson, for tinting *Overmountain Men* photos and line drawings.

Original Copyright 1978 by Pat Alderman
Reprinted with index 1990
ISBN 0-932807-05-4

Printed in the United States of America

3 4 5 6 7 8 9

TABLE OF CONTENTS

NANCY WARD	3
CHEROKEE GOVERNMENT	3
STORM CLOUDS	6
CHILDHOOD	10
INTERIM YEARS	13
FRENCH-INDIAN WAR	15
FORT LOUDOUN	16
TRAGIC AFTERMATH	20
TROUBLES — SURPRISES — TREATIES	25
THE INDIAN AND HIS LAND	29
THE WATAUGA PEOPLE	33
DRAGGING CANOE RAISES HIS TOMAHAWK	37
WAR DRUMS	40
NANCY WARD SENDS WARNING	44
DRAGGING CANOE DEFEATED	45
THE RAVEN OF CHOTA	46
OLD ABRAM AND FORT WATAUGA	46
POWER OF LIFE AND DEATH	47
DESTRUCTION OF MIDDLE, VALLEY, AND LOWER SETTLEMENTS	48
CHRISTAIN'S CAMPAIGN	50
THE LONG ISLAND TREATY	53
THE CHICKAMAUGA RAID	57
DISASTER STRIKES AGAIN	58
BATTLE OF THE HORSES AND HOUNDS (Battle of the Bluffs)	62
NANCY WARD, CHIEFTAINESS	64
CHEROKEE PAWNS	66
HOPEWELL TREATY	67
THE TOMAHAWK STRIKES AGAIN	69
SOUTHWEST TERRITORY	71
DRAGGING CANOE - STRONG MAN OF THE NATION	73
EXCERPTS FROM THE PAST	74
NANCY WARD'S PHILOSOPHY BEARS FRUIT	76
NANCY WARD'S LAST COUNCIL MESSAGE	78
NANCY WARD'S LAST HOME	82
BIBLIOGRAPHY	84

NANCY WARD
Outstanding Cherokee Chieftainess

Nancy Ward was acclaimed *Ghighau* or "Most Honored Woman" of the Cherokee Nation about 1755. Still in her teens and the widowed mother of two children when vaulted into this high office of Chieftainess, she became a strong advocate of human rights for both red men and whites. (This illustration of Nancy by Bernie Andrews was used in the movie production, *The Overmountain People*.)

NANCY WARD

The battle of Taliwa was raging in wild savage fury. Led by their Great War Chief, Oconostota, the Cherokee Warriors were determined to drive the Muskogeans (Creeks) out of North Georgia. The year was 1755; and the Taliwa Battle is said to have been one of the bloodiest ever fought between southeastern tribes.

Nan-ye-hi (Nancy Ward) had accompanied her warrior husband, King Fisher, with this five-hundred-man war party. Crouched beside him behind a protecting log, she was helping King Fisher by chewing the bullets used in his gun. Chewed bullets could rip and mangle the flesh of victims with more deadly results. During one brief moment of exposure King Fisher was mortally wounded; then Nancy, a good marksman and familiar with gun loading, picked up her husband's gun and joined the fight. She fought like a man and stood fast in the battle. Legendary stories hint that Nancy's action was the rallying point for the outnumbered Cherokee and that her entrance into the fight helped turn the tide of the battle. Anyway the Cherokee were victorious; and the Creeks, badly defeated in the Taliwa fight, moved out of North Georgia. This battle climaxed a struggle between the two tribes that began in 1715.

Warriors who fought in the Taliwa battle considered Nancy's act a great heroic deed; and when they returned to Chota, Nancy was acclaimed a great heroine. Stories of her valor in battle were naturally told in home, clan, and passed from town to town. Most likely, dances and festivals were held in her honor. With one accord the ruling Chiefs, Cherokee men and women awarded Nancy the highest honor they could bestow on any woman. She was chosen for the high office of "Ghighau," sometimes called "Most Honored Woman" or "Beloved Woman." It was believed that the Great Spirit often used the voice of the Beloved Woman to speak to the Cherokee. The Honored Woman's words carried great power

The "Honored Woman" title was a lifetime distinction bestowed as an extreme mark of valorous merit. During State Council meetings in the Town House at Chota, Nancy, in her role of Ghighau, sat with the Peace Chief and War Chief in the "holy area" near the ceremonial fire. As head of the Woman's Council, she could speak out and let their opinions be heard. The Female Council did not hesitate to vote to oppose the decisions made by the ruling Headmen if they thought the welfare of the Tribe was at stake.

Though Nancy was in her teens when vaulted into her high position, this honor was ordinarily bestowed on older women who could no longer travel the "war trail." They were awarded this title for outstanding deeds performed when young. It was the only important title Cherokee women could attain.

Legend tells that the Cherokee Nation had been slowly emerging from a petticoat type government; and much of this happened during Nancy Ward's lifetime. That women had long played a prominent role in war and civil councils seems evident. Women are said to have gained fame as warriors with history recording some instances of women on the war trail. One such incident occurred during General Rutherford's expedition against the Cherokee in 1776. Red Warriors took a stand near Wava Gap in the Nantahala Mountains, where a hard fight took place. After the Indians had retreated, a warrior seen peeping from behind a tree was immediately shot and killed. When troops examined the body they discovered it was a woman, painted and dressed like a male warrior with little clothing on her body. Armed with bow and arrows, she had been severely wounded in the thigh. This was the reason she was unable to escape with her party.

Cherokee Government

The Cherokee form of government was a loosely knit union of seventy or eighty tribal towns. These were joined together in a sort of friendly compact of understanding for mutual safety. Each town, community, or settlement was completely independent of another. Early traders have said that individual towns varied in size from twelve family dwellings up to two hundred or more houses per town. Cherokee society was divided into seven clans. Members of each clan lived in practically every town in the Nation. This kinship link formed a network of community ties that made up the National Government. The Nation was organized under a Principal Chief, a Principal Civil Chief who presided during periods of peace and a Principal War Chief who was in charge during War Councils. Headmen or Chiefs from individual towns formed the National Council. This Council met mainly during state ceremonial observances, religious festivals or in times of national emergencies.

The Cherokee People called themselves "Ani-Yunwiya" or "Principal People;" and the Nation was divided into four different settlements. The *Upper Settlement* included towns built along the Little Tennessee, Hiwassee and Tellico Rivers. This section, located in the eastern part of East Tennessee, was called the Overhills.

The *Middle Towns* were settlements in Western North Carolina, situated along the headwaters of the Little Tennessee and Tuckaseegee Rivers.

The *Valley Settlements*, also located in western North Carolina, were spread along the Nottely, upper Hiwassee, and Valley Rivers.

The *Lower Towns* were located on the Tugaloo River and tributaries in northeast Georgia, and others along the Keowee River in South Carolina.

Even though all sections of the Nation spoke the same Cherokee language, there were three different dialects. The Middle and Valley Towns, different from the others, is predominant among the Qualla Indians today. The Lower Town dialect has practically disappeared. The Oklahoma Cherokee language has retained the Overhill sound.

Individual towns had their own Chiefs. Needed assistants, advisors, conjurors and minor officials were chosen for specific duties. This council functioned as a unit in local, military, political and religious rites. One of the first structures to be erected in a Cherokee Town was the Council House. It was a seven-sided building arranged to accommodate all seven clans. Large enough to seat several hundred people, it served as a Religious Temple, Civic Meeting Place and War Council Room.

Timberlake, who spent several months with the Cherokee in 1762, describes the Town House at Chota this way:

> It is raised with wood, and covered over with earth, and has all the appearance of a small mountain at a little distance. It is built in the form of a sugar loaf, and large enough to contain 500 persons, but extremely dark, having, besides the door, which is so narrow that but one at a time can pass, and that after much winding and turning, but one small aperture to let the smoak out, which is so ill contrived, that most of it settles in the roof of the house. Within it has the appearance of an ancient amphitheatre, the seats being raised one above another, leaving an area in the middle, in the center of which stands a fire; the seats of the head warriors are nearest it.

The women had their own clan council. Female members in the local town council chose their own leader, who automatically became a member of the National Women's Council. Nancy Ward, as "Ghighau" or "Greatly Honored Woman," thus became the Chief Woman of the Cherokee Female Council. Nancy was the last woman of the Cherokee Nation to hold this office. Some authorities have mentioned that Nancy Ward helped lead her people through some difficult years, furnishing leadership and advice that helped bridge the gap between their savage state of living and white man's civilization.

Nancy was born 1737-1738 in Chota, Capital Town of the Cherokee. Her mother is said to have been Tame Doe, a niece of "Old Hop," called "Cherokee Emperor" by the whites, and actually Principal Chief. One of Tame Doe's brothers was Attakullakulla, Great Solon and Peace Chief. He is rated by historians as the most celebrated and influential Indian among Southern Indian Tribes during his time of leadership. He was named "Little Carpenter" by the whites because of his uncanny ability in fitting parts of a peace treaty into a good diplomatic document. The Carpenter stood out in his state craft, diplomacy and leadership. Oconostota, the War Chief during much of the 18th century, has been rated as one of their greatest. Many historians have suggested that the Cherokee story of that century could be built around these two personalities. During this same period the Cherokee were considered the most civilized tribe among neighboring southeastern tribes.

Nancy and King Fisher had two children, Catherine and Little Fellow. Sometime during the mid 1750s Nancy married Bryant Ward, an English Trader who had come to Chota. There is a legend that Nancy and Bryant were married in a civil ceremony. This could easily be so. This union gave birth to Elizabeth, shortened by usage to Betsy. The marriage also gave Nancy the English name *Nancy Ward* that would later be recorded as an outstanding historic personality in Cherokee-Tennessee-American journals.

Nancy's father, who has little importance in the story except for being her father, is said to have been a Delaware Chief. Emmett Starr, Cherokee historian, says that Nancy Ward was a full-blooded Cherokee. Jack Hildebrand, great-grandson of Nancy Ward, says that Nancy's father was a Delaware Chief who married the sister of Attakullakulla and, according to Indian custom, had become a member of her tribal clan. The Delawares were considered the original settlers of the Atlantic Seaboard and were called the "Grandfather" Indians. They called themselves "Lenni-Lennape," very important people.

The seven clans on which the Cherokee Nation was founded were: Ani-Waya, Wolf Clan, of which Nancy Ward was a member; Ani-Kawi, Deer People; Ani-Tsi-S-Kwa, Bird People; Ani-Wodi, Paint People; Ani-Ga-To-Ge-Wi, Wild Potato People; Ani-Gi-Lo-Hi, Long Hair People; and Ani-Sa-Ho-Ni, Blue People.

In the matriarchial clan background, their basis of family life, the women had more matrimonial rights than did the men. The dwelling and its contents belonged to the wife; children belonged to the mother's clan; the husband became a member of his wife's clan at marriage. Cherokee wedding rites were simple and not too binding. One mentioned custom was for the bride to present an ear of corn to the prospective groom as a symbol of her willingness to be a good wife. If the male was receptive he would present the lady with a leg of venison, which was a promise that he would provide the family with food. The Cherokee had no laws against adultery. The women had full liberties and could, with Amazon-like freedom, divorce bad-tempered husbands at their own pleasure.

Nancy has been described as a strikingly beautiful woman, with a tall erect figure, prominent nose, regular features, tawny complexion, long silken black hair, and large piercing black eyes. All reports indicate an imperious but kindly disposition along with a queenly and majestic character.

A story is told that because the texture of her skin, while young, was tinted like a pink-reddish wild rose petal, she was given the nickname "Tsistuna-gis-ke" (Wild Rose). This flower once flourished in the Overhill Country. The Cherokee Rose is the official flower of Georgia and is sometimes associated with the name Nancy Ward.

One of Nancy Ward's duties as "Honored Woman" was to prepare the sacred "Black Drink." This seems to have been a ritual used by Southeastern Tribes, especially the Creeks

Nancy Ward's position vested her with supreme pardoning power: the right to pardon, release, or condemn any captive held by the Cherokee. This was a power not granted to either the powerful Peace Chief or War Chief of the Nation.

and Cherokee. The celebrated Black Drink was a concoction made from the leaves, tops and shoots of shrub Ilex vomitoria, a member of the Holly family. We know the shrub by its common name the Winterberry. The caffeine in the plant produces a stimulant. A strong infusion of the plant juices in liquids produced a narcotic once used by conjurers to evoke ecstasies. No Indian was allowed to partake of the purifying drink unless he had proved himself a brave warrior.

Timberlake describes its ceremonial preparation and use from actual observation. Nancy Ward was the head Ghighau during his stay with the Cherokee, 1761-1762:

> A vessel of their own, made from clay was set on the fires, round which stood several gourds filled with river water, which was poured into the pot; this done, there arose one of the Beloved Women, who, opening a deer-skin bag filled with roots and herbs, took out a small handful of something like fine salt; part of which she threw on the headman's [Chief's] seat, and part into the fire close to the pot; she then took out the wing of a swan, and after flourishing it over the pot, stood fixed for near a minute as she mumbled an ancient chant, then reached again into the deer-skin pouch. She withdrew branches of the yaupon shrub which she cast into the boiling water of the twenty-gallon pot. After this she returned to her seat.

Later the Indians assembled to partake of the drink; the house was full. They danced nearly an hour around the pot; then one of them took a gourd and dipped a drink, after which each one took his turn with the gourd.

Timberlake says in his *Memoirs* that the "Black Drink" ritual might be ranked among the Cherokee religious ceremonies. Much preparation is made for its observance. He continues:

> Starting several mornings before the day set for its observance, the Conjuror climbs to the top of the Town House each morning and frightens away apparitions and evil spirits with dreadful howling, yelling and hallowing.

The "Black Drink" was used as a purification-from-sin ritual. It was part of certain State Council Ceremonials. The sacred "Holy Drink" was served during certain parts of the corn and harvest festivals. All were religious related.

Nancy Ward, performing one of her duties as Ghighau, is said to have prepared and served the Black Drink for the warriors in their purification rites during July 1776 before the War Parties left the Overhills to attack the Nolichucky, Watauga and Holston settlements.

STORM CLOUDS

Foreboding storm signals cast threatening shadows over the heart and security of the Cherokee culture years before the birth of either Nancy Ward or her cousin Dragging Canoe. Events were taking shape that would affect both their adult lives. These two future Cherokee leaders would, years hence, face conditions and situations undreamt by their forebears.

For about two hundred years after Desoto passed through the lower part of their Nation, the Cherokee people are said to have lived a normal, happy primitive life style. They became the dominant tribe of the southeast. A congenial, self-reliant, self-sustaining people, they lived a leisurely lazy-like sort of life. Forests stocked with game furnished meat for food and skins for clothing and blankets. Rivers and creeks teemed with fish and fresh-water clams. Farming supplied corn, beans, squash, pumpkin and potatoes. Wild plants furnished many other edibles. Tobacco for their ritual pipes was plentiful and easy to grow. Craftsmanship supplied bows and arrows, blow guns and other needed weapons.

Pots and cooking vessels with intricate stamped designs were molded from native clay. With flint knives they carved their stone pipes out of steatite. Beautiful pipes, large and small, were shaped in human, animal and bird figures. Wood carving furnished ceremonial masks and many other needed items. Their basket weaving was artistic in design and practical in size and shape. Native ability in utilizing everything in their environment supplied life's necessities and made them independent. Most of their vast claimed territory was needed for hunting, fishing, farming, collecting wild roots, nuts, salad greens and medicinal herbs. Indians maintained an ecological balance with nature; and their population somehow kept a simple balance with plant life, water life and the animals of the forests.

It is pretty well established that Woodland People were the earliest Appalachian mountaineers. Their ancient village sites can be found in many areas of the Southern Highlands.

The Cherokee, said to have been long-time inhabitants of the southeast, most likely originated from the late Woodland traditions. Cherokee culture is said to have been

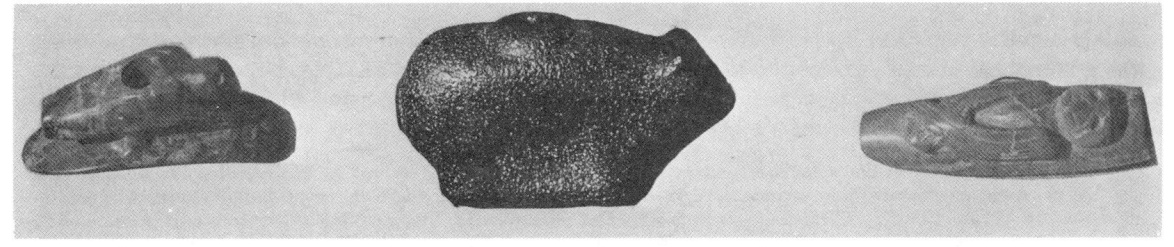
Hand carved stone pipes were made in bird, animal, and human shapes.

predominantly of Mississippian influence. The Cherokee were the first known Southern Appalachian Mountain dwellers of historic record.

Many authorities have expressed belief that pre-white Cherokee culture, craft and art forms were as rich and colorful as that of the better known western tribes. The penetration of European culture into the inner circles of Cherokee life gradually disturbed, distorted, and obscured much of their cultural patterns, craftsmanship and life styles before it could be intelligently observed and recorded.

Pre-white Cherokee seem to have lived a normal, simple, uncomplicated, satisfying, primitive life style. Simple taboos and purification rites before, during, and after menses or pregnancy; nursing babies for two years; and men absent during long periods, either fighting or hunting, all aided in controlling the birth rate. The average Cherokee couple had two children. Their population increase was large enough to insure tribal continuation but not to overpopulate. Individual quality seemed more important than numbers.

During certain seasons dances were held nearly every night. Some were social, like the *feather dance*, when both men and women participated. Others pantomimed ancient tribal history and legends. Many dances demonstrated how the men hunted large and small animals or waged war against their enemies. With certain dance styles they took care of their poor and needy, the widows and orphans.

From Timberlake's recorded visit to the Overhills in 1762 comes this account:

> The Indians have a particular method of relieving the poor, which I rank among the most laudable of their religious ceremonies. . . When any of their people are hungry, as they term it, or in distress, orders are issued out by the headmen for a war-dance, at which all the fighting men and warriors assemble; but here contrary to all their other dances, one only dances at a time, who, after hopping and capering for near a minute, with a tomahawk in his hand, gives a small whoop, at which signal the music stops till he relates the manner of taking his first scalp, and concludes his narration by throwing on a large skin, spread for that purpose, a string of wampum, piece of plate, wire, paint, lead, or any thing he can most conveniently spare; after which the music strikes up, and he proceeds in the same manner through all his war-like actions; then another takes his place and the ceremony lasts till all the warriors and fighting men have related their exploits. The stock thus raised, after paying the musicians, is divided among the poor.

During 1783-1784 Martin Schneider was visiting in the Overhill Towns with the idea of establishing a Moravian Mission there. From his diary has been transcribed this report as taken from the Moravian Archives:

> This evening there is to be continued here in Chota a great Dancing of Women, which is to be continued four (4) Evenings. I was told that twice a year or oftener such a Dancing is appointed in every Town, to which no one has Leave to come, except he (or she) brings at least one Skin. And thus they get every time a pretty number of skins together, who are made use of for the poor who suffer want.

Many fundamental, prehistoric beliefs, customs and games have continued on into the 20th century. One was their stick-ball game. Every town had a special playing field. The game, somewhat similar to modern Lacrosse, was and is an extremely rough game. Even so, both men and women played; and quite often some of the participants left the contest with a broken arm or leg. This game might have been a sort of substitute for war, as it offered an outlet for violent and aggressive emotions.

Then came the intrusion of the European trader with the white man's wares. Iron and brass kettles began to replace homemade pottery. Time-honored native dress styles were discarded for European made clothing. Inherited weapons were laid aside or supplemented with the white man's guns, powder and lead. The stone tomahawk was swapped for the iron hatchet.

Goods usually supplied by traders included matched coats (a combination blanket and overcoat), blankets, shirts, petticoats, stockings, ribbons, bracelets, anklets, beads, bells, scissors, awls, pipes, vermillion paint, salt, looking glasses, steel needles and clothing. Hunters and warriors wanted the white man's guns, powder, bullets and his iron tomahawks.

A real modern innovation was this European made pipe-tomahawk described by Timberlake: The hammer side of the head was hollow like the bowl of a pipe. A hole was drilled through the wood handle lengthwise to connect with the hollow bowl. The opening at bottom end of the handle was fitted with a brass mouthpiece. The sharp blade opposite the pipe bowl made an excellent cutting tool for scalping or building a fire. A few of the new-styled tomahawks were fitted with a spear-like top that could be used like a sabre. Thus a warrior had his pipe, tomahawk and spear in one convenient tool. They were expert at throwing this weapon with deadly accuracy at man or beast some distance away.

As the volume of European supplies increased, the more the natives wanted and depended on this source. They practically stopped making their own; and this tended to make them lazy and improvident. Traders hauled their wares into the nation with pack horses. The trips to Charles Town and back to the Overhill towns sometimes took three months or more. Traders, as required, married Cherokee women, establishing homes and families in their headquarters towns. They built storehouses to protect their pelts and wares. Gradually, as the Cherokee forsook and neglected their own craft and customs, they became dependent and enslaved to the traders' demands. They bartered their individual and tribal independence for the white man's wares and ways. The entrance of European culture into the Cherokee life style forced the Indians to face two different worlds.

English traders began penetrating Cherokee country about 1690. Listed among early names plying that trade were Anthony Deane, Cornelius Dougherty, Eleazar Wiggam, Alexander Long, Ludovich Grant, Daniel Jenkinson, David Dowie, Joseph Cooper, Gregory Haines, Joseph Barker, William Hatton, James Dauge, Thomas Goodale and Joseph Biles. The trader-Indian relationship was on a credit basis. Traders would advance Indians requested supplies; and the Indian hunter secured deer hides to pay his debt. Agreed prices were set by Indians and whites. A gun could be bought for thirty-five deer skins; a duffle blanket for sixteen; a calico petticoat for fourteen; thirty bullets, a knife, a string of beads, a pair of scissors (or twelve flints) for one skin.

James Adair, in his "History of the American Indians," says that most families in the Cherokee Nation had from two to a dozen horses. There were several excellent breeds until the beginning of the late wars. Starvation then forced the Indians to use the greater part of them for food. Legend says that a trader named Dougherty taught the Cherokee warriors how to steal horses from Virginia plantations. Most of the white traders living in the nation are said to have maintained a large number of horses for hauling goods and trading. They built their corrals outside the towns away from crop fields.

Many early South Carolina fortunes were built on the Indian fur trade. The Carolina Colonies were also aware that their safety depended on friendly relations with the Cherokee who occupied the back door to their settlements. In 1715 the Cherokee population was estimated to be about eleven to twelve thousand, about half of them warriors.

The South Carolina merchants, disturbed by inroads the French were making on the Indian fur trade, decided to hold a treaty and talk the Cherokee into a closer commitment. Governor Nicholson of South Carolina invited the Cherokees to a council at Charles Town. He wanted to woo the Indian fur trade away from the French traders plying the Mississippi Valley. At the conclusion of the 1721 Treaty the Indians had ceded a fifty-square-mile tract of land between the Santee, Saluda, and Edisto Rivers. The Treaty also secured a trade agreement with the Cherokees for most of their furs. The signing of this treaty of allegiance and making this first cession of land to the English was another step toward the loss of their culture, homeland and eventual removal to the West.

Nine years after this first cession was signed by Cherokee Chiefs, one of the most bizarre events of history occurred. Alexander Cuming came to America in hopes of building a fortune. After most of his schemes had failed, he decided to leave Charles Town and visit the Cherokee Nation. Taking advantage of the red man's ignorance while there, Sir Alexander Cuming pulled off an amazing stunt. This feat influenced the Cherokee Nation for many decades. Standing outside a Council Hall where some three hundred Indians were meeting, Cuming prepared a cunning coup. Concealing guns and a sword under his long coat he entered the Council Hall; and with eloquent words, veiled in threats, he had all the Headmen present kneel and swear allegiance to the King of England. To make this stunt credible, he practically forced all the white traders present to sign their names as witnesses. Messengers were then sent into all the towns of the Overhill Country, the Middle Towns, Valley, and the Lower Towns, telling all the Chiefs and Headmen to meet at Nequassee so many days hence. Cuming planned to have these leaders swear allegiance to the English Crown. (Nequassee was located near the present site of Franklin, North Carolina.)

Sir Alexander Cuming had no authority for this performance. He merely seized this course of action to gain prominence for himself. With dreams of becoming important as the great benefactor of the red man, he made a grand tour of the Cherokee Nation in an attempt to set up his Kingdom. At Tellico he maneuvered to have Maytoy named Emperor.

Cuming's exploit reached its climax at Nequassee April 3, 1730. Determined to make all England conscious of his great achievement, he worked out a plan to take several young warriors to London to personally meet the King. The Indians were hesitant about making such an unknown and dangerous journey.

Eleazar Wiggam, an English trader, was the close friend of a young warrior called Chuconnunta. As Cuming's scheme to take some Cherokee men back to London with him was not going so well, he asked Wiggam to help. Wiggam finally persuaded Ukwanequa, called Chuconnunta, to make the trip. This young Indian brave was later to be known as Attakullakulla (The Little Carpenter), Dragging Canoe's father and Nancy Ward's uncle. The Little Carpenter left this account of the final selection of those making the trip overseas. (Cumings had said it would be better if others went.) From South Carolina Magazine of History comes this quote:

> After some questions were asked about England and how far it might be to it, not one of our people would go... At night Mr. Wiggam the interpreter, came to the house where I (Attakullakulla) was and told me that the Warrior Cumings had a particular favour for me, and that if I would consent to go he would be indifferent whether any other went... and Mr. Wiggam pressed me very much to accept of his invitation... He assured me that the distance was very much magnified and that I should be back by the end of summer or at least sometime in the fall, upon which assurance I agreed to go... Early next morning one of our people came to me and said that I should not go alone for he would accompany me and that he knew two or three others that he could persuade to go; accordingly they were spoken to and agreed, and we immediately got ready and soon started off.

Seven young Cherokee men made the trip. Only two were Chiefs at the time. Six had come to Charles Town as official representatives of the Nation. The seventh was Onokanowin, who asked permission to make the trip shortly before sailing time. The seven were: Ounaconoa (Onakanowin, Oukounaco), Prince Sealilosken or Skalilosken (Kitagista or Kellagustah), Kollannah or Kilonah (The Raven of Nequassee), Oukah Ulah or O.K. Oukah Ulah (Okeah Ulah), Tathtowe or Tiftowe, Clogoittah, Ukwaneequa or Chuconnunta (Attakullakulla, The Little Carpenter). The arrival of the young Red Men in London caused quite a commotion. They were wined and dined by Royalty, with King George II inviting them as his guests in the palace where they were permitted to kiss his hands and those of his two sons. They presented to the King their Indian crown, made of 'possum fur dyed red, and decorated with scalps and eagle tails. The King paid the expenses of the Indians during their extended trip. Mutual pledges were given by the two nations. The Cherokees promised that no other white people would be allowed to settle in their country, and that they would trade with no one else but King George's representatives. They also promised to aid Great Britain in time of war.

From left to right are Ounaconoa, Prince Skalilosken, Kollanna, Oukah Ulah, Tathtowe, Clogoittah, and Ukwaneequa. *(From the British Museum.)*

Kitagista, Oconostota's brother, also called the Prince, was spokesman for the group and made the following speech (abbreviated):

> We are come hither from a dark and mountainous country, but we are now in a place of light. The crown of our nation is different from that which our father, King George, wears but it is all one. The chain of friendship shall be carried to our people. We look upon King George as the sun, and our father, and upon ourselves as his children; for though you are white and we are red, our hands and hearts are joined together. When we have acquainted our people with what we have seen, our children from generation to generation will remember it. In war we shall always be as one with you. The great King's enemies shall be our enemies. His people and ours shall always be as one, and we shall die together.

The trip and visit consumed an entire year. Loaded with presents and honors the Cherokee warriors returned to their homeland May 11, 1731; but because of financial difficulties, Sir Alexander Cuming did not return with them. The Cherokees had gained a Great White Father but had mortgaged their freedom.

CHILDHOOD

Nothing is known about Nancy Ward's childhood; but her experiences and training must have been similar to other children of her tribe, clan and time. It is said that a warm, congenial relationship existed among clan families, expecially those with children.

Nancy lived most of her life in Chota, long time capital of the Cherokee nation. She belonged to the Wolf Clan, one of the most distinguished of the seven Cherokee tribal clans. Nancy was born into one of the first families of that tribe. Her mother's kinship to many prominent Chiefs and Headmen endowed Nancy with as strong a claim to royal blood as Cherokee culture afforded.

Cherokee education was partly accomplished by imitation, repetition and observation. Teaching was done by parents and older men and women or specialists. These veterans quite often were the grandpas and grandmas who were too old to hunt or fight. When called on to baby-sit, they entertained the youngsters with Cherokee stories, legends and lore—all instructive and exciting.

The Cherokee had no written language yet. All legends, tribal history, lore, ceremonial rituals and routines had to be passed on to the next generation orally. Because of this, much of early Cherokee culture has been obscure.

Bright children were chosen early in life to learn certain crafts, trades, professions, and train for chieftainship roles. Leaders of each generation had to pass their knowledge, routines and experience on the the next. This included dancing teachers, musicians, doctors, geologists, biologists, craftsmen, potters, and all phases of special careers. Long hours and periods of fasting were spent by the trainees, learning endurance along with the details and functions of religious, social and state ceremonies.

Cherokee boys and girls were taught from childhood to respect the elderly. The Patriarchs were called "the old ones" and referred to as the wise old men. Elders of the clan and tribe spent much time with youngsters, teaching them ages-old legends of their people which were the colorful part of their past. They educated youth with recitals of ancient myths and rituals, stories of heroic deeds accomplished by past revered leaders and warriors.

Cherokee children learned in this manner the story of Kanati, the first Cherokee man and patron of all hunters; the legend of Selu, the first Cherokee woman; and the saint or spirit "Agawela" who gave them corn.

In this way the youth learned about many Cherokee traditional beliefs, one of which centered around the Moon Deity. The crescent shapes of the moon determined the time of all religious festivals. They were taught that the world was created in the fall season when corn and nuts were ripe and ready to eat. Their year began with October's new moon.

Much of Cherokee spiritual mythology was centered around symbols of the sacred seven. The Cherokee's universe had seven heavens, seven directions, seven clans, seven great ceremonies in their religious observances, seven sacred trees.

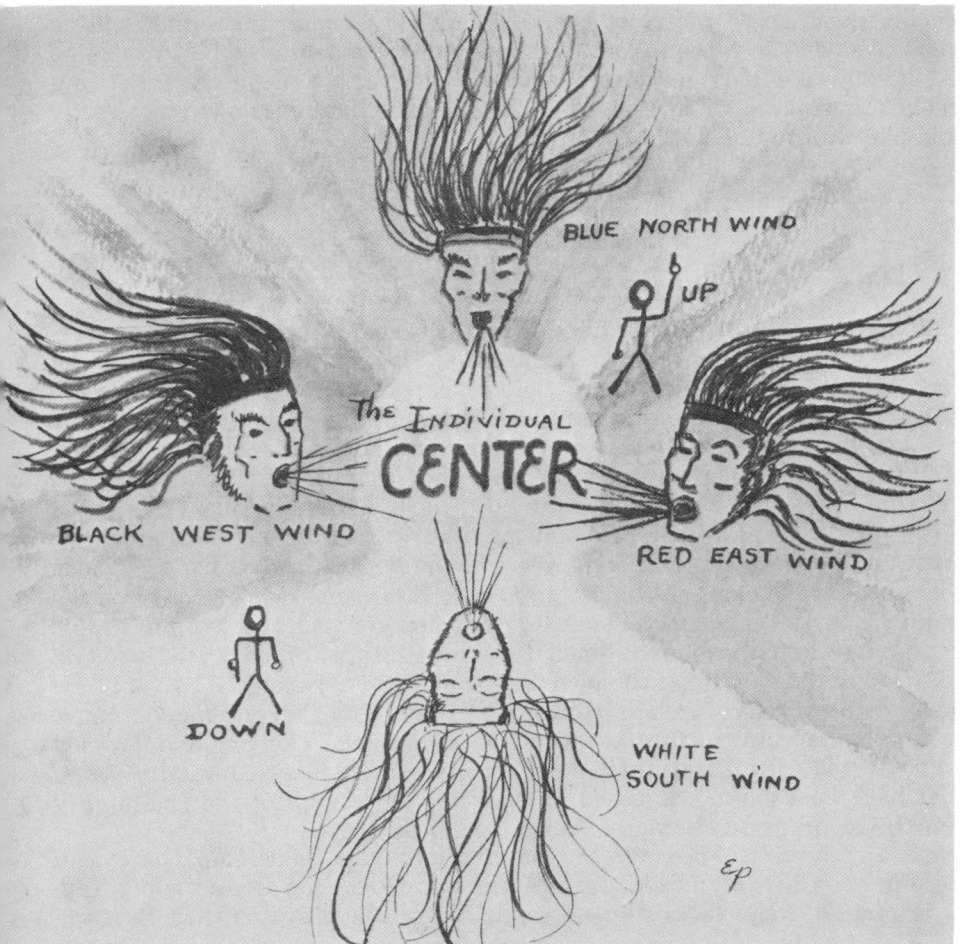

Cherokee believed in seven directions:
(1) *Here* where I stand is the center of the universe;
2) *Up* where the heavenly bodies live;
(3) *Down* where the evil spirits stay;
(4) *East* from whence comes the winds directed by the red spirit to give us victory in war;
(5) *North* from where the cold blue winds blow the spirit of defeat;
(6) *West* winds on which rides the black specters of sickness and death;
(7) White gentle winds of the *South* which bring messages of peace.

One can imagine with what awe the youngsters must have listened to the mythical story of how their beloved country was formed. How the earth in the beginning was flat, soft and wet. A Great Buzzard, Grandfather of all Buzzards, once flew over the earth when it was soft. He flew over the country of the Cherokee with wings spread so wide it shadowed the sun. The Great Bird, tiring from its long journey, swooped down close to the ground. His mighty wings scooped up miles of soft dirt, leaving deep valleys in his wake with every sweep of his flight. The upward lift of his wings piled the dirt in high mounds which formed the mountains.

Another myth tells how fire was brought to the earthlings. Lightning, the servant of thunder, had placed fire, the protector of human beings, in a great sycamore hollow stump. This stump was located on a great island surrounded by a large body of water. Many animals volunteered to swim or fly to the island and bring a spark of fire from the stump to their human friends. The Raven, named Colonah, was first to try. In attempting to get a live coal from the stump his feathers were scorched. He has been black ever since. The owls were next to undertake the mission. The small Screech Owl, called Wa-hu-hu, and the Great Horned Owl, U-gu-ku, flew to the island. The heat burned their eyes so badly, they must hide during the day and fly by night. The little blacksnake, Uk-suhi, and the Great Black Snake, Gulegi, swam to the island. The little snake found a hole and crawled into the stump. The hot ashes nearly burned him to death before he could escape. The Great Black Snake climbed the stump and fell inside. Before he was able to wiggle out he was also burned black like his little brother. The little water spider with a pack on his back swam to the island. He put a spark in his pack and brought it back to the main land.

Another fable which small Indians surely must have enjoyed was about the race between the rabbit and the terrapin. The course was laid out across three hills. The slow terrapin knew he had to resort to strategy to beat the swift rabbit. The terrapin posted four of his relatives—one on each hill and one at the starting line. As they all looked alike no one, not even the rabbit, could tell them apart. The race started, and the rabbit quickly left his opponent behind. When he reached the top of the first hill he was surprised to see the terrapin already there. He increased his speed as he raced for the next hill. On topping the second hill he couldn't believe what he saw. The terrapin had beat him again. Faster the rabbit ran as he raced for the third hill and was almost outdone to find the slow racer already there. Leaving his opponent behind again, he raced for the finish line. Lo and behold, the terrapin was already crossing the line and had won the race.

One of the most lasting results of the trip to London by the seven Cherokee was the impression made on the youngest man in the party, Attakullakulla. The greatness and power of the British seems to have molded and dominated the diplomatic policies of Attakullakulla, who became a Chief during the 1730s. These impressions were evident in his talks and actions during the remainder of his years. The Carpenter's philosophy and hopes of achieving peaceful solutions with the whites seems to have been passed on to his protege, Nancy Ward.

One can imagine the young Nancy sitting near her Uncle Attakullakulla (The Little Carpenter) listening to him tell and retell stories about his trip to England. This great experience of the Carpenter happened seven or eight years before her birth. How her eyes must have shone as he told about the big man-of-war ship, *The Fox*, breasting the high waves on the Big Water; the big guns that could roar with such a loud voice; the pageantry of the King's throne room; the great notables with whom he dined; the strong display of red-coated soldiers, all armed with guns; the formal signing of the pledge of friendship between the two nations.

Both Nancy and her cousin Tsi.yuGansi.ni (Dragging Canoe, The Carpenter's son) must have received many lasting impressions from these recitals. Nancy was likely more impressed by the diplomatic image created, judging from the direction her life followed in later years. Tsi.yuGansi.ni must have been more impressed by stories and descriptions of the mighty armies, the power of the big guns on the warships that ruled the waves.

Nancy Ward became an advocate of peace as she matured into tribal leadership. Her cousin Dragging Canoe became the Cherokee patriot savage warrior who spread terror among frontier settlers. These are purely conjectural suggestions based on the direction their lives followed in later life.

INTERIM YEARS

The two decades between 1730 and 1750 were filled with events which would greatly influence the Cherokee Nation during the last half of the 18th century. Among them were: the voyage of the seven Cherokee to London; the birth of Tsi.yuGansi.ni (Dragging Canoe), son of Attakullakulla; the arrival of Nanye-hi (Nancy Ward), born to the sister of Attakullakulla and given the name that signified *One who goes about* (from Nunne-hi, the legendary name of the *Spirit People* of Cherokee mythology). Also, the gradual disintegration of the matrilineal clan-tribal system of government had started. Clan kinship, which existed in practically every Cherokee town, was the slender thread that had held the Nation together for centuries.

Another influence that would bring problems to the Nation was the arrival of Christain Priber, a Jesuit priest. Priber established his home in the town of Great Tellico sometime before 1736. Adopting the Indian manner of living as well as dress, he espoused hopes of establishing a *Communistic Republic* in the Nation. Priber has been identified as a representative from the French; and he strongly influenced the Tellico chiefs, who later wanted to lead the Cherokee to a French-Cherokee alliance and oppose the English. The Indians liked Priber, but it is doubtful if they understood his philosophy and teachings. He was eventually captured by English traders and later died in a Georgia jail.

Chota is thought to have become the capital of the Nation about 1730. The location of the capital town changed, with the selection of a new Principal Chief, to his resident town. In 1715 the Cherokee capital was Tugaloo, located in northeastern Georgia. When Colonel George Chicken visited the Nation in 1725, the capital was Tenasi, near Chota. (Tenasi is the Cherokee town name from which the state of Tennessee and its main river are named.)

An epidemic of smallpox swept through the Nation during 1738-1739. This scourge, which destroyed half the population, was contracted from a slave ship which unloaded its cargo in Charles Town harbor. Nancy Ward somehow escaped the dreaded disease; but young Dragging Canoe and Oconostota, the Great War Chief, were not so fortunate. Both survived, but later records describe their faces as pock-scarred.

Smallpox was a contagious disease about which the Cherokee Adawehi (Medicine Men) knew nothing. Having no previous experience or known treatment for this malady, they told their people this sickness was brought on them as a punishment by the Great Spirit for the evil ways of the young. The Medicine Man attempted to treat the disease several ways. One was by giving a sweat bath in the *Hot House*, followed by a cold plunge in the river. This proved to be a fatal remedy.

The "Hot House" was a small hut which joined the main dwelling, with the floor dug three or four feet below ground level. The walls and roof were tight, except for the small hole left in the roof for smoke to escape. Wood pole or cane couches were built around the wall for sleeping; and a fire, on the floor fireplace near the center, often burned day and night. It is said that the room would become so hot that little clothing, if any, could be worn even on the coldest day of winter. Every Indian dwelling had a "Hot House" for use as winter quarters. Inside and outside views of "Hot House" are from the re-created *Oconaluftee Cherokee Indian Village* of 200 years ago, in Cherokee, North Carolina. Photos by John Parris courtesy Cherokee Historical Association.

Another situation was to prove disastrous for the Cherokee during the first half of the 18th century. The demand for animal skins to pay their debts to English traders increased yearly; and hunting was changing from a fun sport, to get meat for the family, to a hard business proposition. The warriors wanted the traders' guns, powder and lead; and the women perhaps nagged to get iron pots, bright-colored stockings, ribbons, petticoats and other items. Indian hunters forsook their ancient ways and customs in protecting nature's balance in the animal world. They began to kill for profit rather than food.

English records and general estimates have come up with some interesting figures. From 1699 to 1715, an average of 54,000 deer skins per year were shipped from the Charles Town port. By 1748 this number had increased to 160,000 per year. From 1739 to 1759, it is said, over a million and a half deer skins were shipped through the Charles Town port. This big kill, using European guns, almost exhausted the deer population in the South. During the third quarter of the 18th century, Cherokee hunters were complaining that they had to travel a long distance northward to find game.

Cherokee men are said to have been slightly above medium height. Their complexion was olive with a copperish tint. The *red man* label was given to Indians by Europeans because of the red paint used on their faces and bodies when on the warpath or during certain ceremonial dances. The hairless Indian is, in fact, a fiction. The hair was plucked from their bodies by the roots, using clam shell tweezers until metal pullers were introduced. White traders taught them how to use the razor and looking glass; and no decent warrior would be caught without his mirror. Feathers often dangled from a patch of hair left on the head; and a loin cloth girded the mid-section. At home the male wore English-made hunting shirts, cloth leggings, and deerskin moccasins. A large mantle-type long coat was draped over the shoulders. When on the war trail or off hunting, these belongings were left at home. Warriors wore only the barest necessities when fighting. Some writers have said that Cherokee warriors, *man for man*, (and for that matter, Indian warriors of all tribes) proved that they were about the best fighters ever produced by the human race.

Cherokee women are said to have been tall, slim, and graceful. Their complexion was fairer than that of the men. They wore their hair long, sometimes hanging midway down their legs, and they used the red hulls of the sumac berries to make a toilet solution to preserve its blackness and splendor. They either braided or clubbed their hair; and traders furnished bright colored ribbons to adorn the braids. Women also plucked the hair from their bodies, leaving only the hair of their head and eyelashes. By the middle of the 18th century, their dress had a European look and style.

Cherokee religious ceremonials and rituals were so closely interwoven with their civil and social observances that it was hard for outsiders to separate the two. Their religious beliefs were as important and necessary to them as food and water. Seasonal, annual ceremonies and dances were aids to the Indian's understanding of nature and they guided him in efforts to build a more orderly community. When traveling wilderness trails, he might have used a deer skin as a prayer rug while the smoke from his campfire wafted his prayers skyward.

Cherokee civilization, as measured by European standards, was uncivilized, unrefined, and barbaric. White man's civilization as judged by Cherokee thinking was biased. Cherokee leaders were mostly chosen on merit; a warrior had to win his laurels. White leaders were selected by party prejudice. Whites sold their high titles of war and government to the highest bidder. Cherokee people gave them to brave patriotic warriors who fought for their country. Another Cherokee observation was that poor white people could not afford justice, while rich knaves gave large sums to have their black actions painted white. White men's laws condemned the little rogues but spared the big ones.

The English themselves were encroaching on Indian land daily. Cherokee hunting grounds were being despoiled and depleted. Indians were beginning to realize that they were losing their lands, but not understanding why and how. The Cherokee, as did all other Eastern Indian tribes, held a peculiar affection and tenderness for their forests, lakes, creeks, and rivers. These were the lands where their fathers were born and buried. Indians, living in their wilderness seclusion, had little comprehension or understanding of international political forces which were closing in from all sides.

FRENCH-INDIAN WAR

Nancy Ward was acclaimed Cherokee's "Honored Woman" just a year or two after the American phase of the war between France and England began. Nancy's role in the State Council during those early years must have been mostly functionary, as she was very young and inexperienced in affairs of state. She must have done much listening and learning as the elder chiefs (especially her two mentors—Attakullakulla, Peace Chief, and Oconostota, War Chief) discussed Cherokee problems.

The American phase of the French-English war was a power struggle for control of the Mississippi Valley, sometimes called the heartland of America. Ironically, both European nations were trying to use the natives who owned the land to fight their colonial war. Both France and England knew that control of the land lying between the Appalachian Mountains and the Mississippi River was essential to the establishment of a great Colonial Empire. Officials of both nations were also aware that they must deal with the Indian tribes who claimed the land. Shrewd representatives from both sides were constantly visiting among southeastern tribes, courting their friendship and support.

The Cherokee Nation became a real political pawn in this power struggle. They were the strongest tribe in the southeast, and their strategic geographical location made them very important to both countries.

The year 1755 was a desperate one for the British Colonials as the French were winning battles on every front. Colonel George Washington, then a British officer, was valiantly trying to defend Virginia's western frontiers. He repeatedly asked that Virginia officials enlist Indian warriors to offset the strength of the French-allied Indian fighters.

Virginia's Royal Governor Dinwiddie was urgently trying to persuade the Cherokee to send warriors to Virginia's aid, but the Cherokee Chiefs refused because they were unwilling to leave their home towns unprotected. Many of the French-allied tribes were traditional enemies, so the Cherokee Chiefs insisted that forts be built within their nation and garrisoned to protect their women and children.

Eventually, in spite of jealous bickering between Governor Dinwiddie of Virginia and Governor Glenn of South Carolina, forts were built. Fort Prince George, on the banks of the Keowee River near the lower towns, was the first. North Carolina officials erected Fort Dobbs. (Mooney says this fort was located about twenty miles west of present Salisbury, North Carolina.) Finally Fort Loudoun was erected on the banks of the Little Tennessee River near Chota.

There was bitter feuding between the officials of Virginia and South Carolina over the profitable fur trade with the Indians. South Carolina officials were the first to seriously consider building forts in the Nation. Another serious consideration was the fact that the Cherokee occupied territory at their back door, and safety of the colony depended on friendly relations.

An early attempt to win the Cherokee friendship for Virginia was attempted in June 1756 when Dinwiddie sent tools, supplies, and some sixty men to build a fort at Chota. By midsummer of that year a log stockade, one hundred feet square, was erected about a mile from the Capital Town. Major Andrew Lewis, in charge of this  mission, had hoped to lead several hundred warriors back to Virginia to join their armed forces. Less than a dozen went. Virginia, short of armed men, asked North Carolina to garrison the new fort. They refused; and this nameless fort, within the Cherokee Overhill country, was never garrisoned. The Cherokee, afraid that some enemy tribe might take over the empty stockade, destroyed the structure.

In-fighting between the officials of the Carolinas and Virginia, and their arrogant attitudes toward the Indians, were straining English-Cherokee relations. Constant encroachment by South Carolina settlers on the hunting lands of the Lower Cherokee Settlements was causing much resentment in that section of the Nation. The only reason that Cherokee-English ties of friendship lasted was the Indians' total dependence on English supplies.

News that the French were planning to build a fort near Great Tellico aroused the South Carolinians to action. Mankiller, one of the strong Chiefs of Tellico Town, favored the French; and in a speech before the National Council he urged the Chiefs to join the French alliance. In an effort to beat the French, Fort Loudoun was built in 1756 and garrisoned the next year.

During 1757-1758, bands of Cherokee warriors began leaving for Virginia to aid the British against the French. They had been promised pay for enemy scalps and that all needed supplies would be furnished. Moravian records at Old Salem (Winston-Salem, North Carolina) mention that bands of warriors were constantly passing to and fro through their community. It is estimated that about seven hundred Cherokee warriors went to Virginia's aid during 1757-1758.

From the very start, there was friction between British officers and the Indians. To most officers the Indians were something to be bought and sold and, when their usefulness was over, discarded. General Washington is reported to have said, "The British regulars and their officers were totally unfit to deal or work with Indians."

Many incidents occurred that fed the fires of bitter resentment already existing among several Chiefs who had trustingly led their warriors to Virginia's aid. For instance, when a scouting detail returned to headquarters camp for needed supplies, there was no interpreter present to explain their needs; so their requests were refused. Another party had left their horses at headquarters; but when they returned and asked for their mounts, the officers in charge refused to let them have any horses. One party was jailed for ten days, until Ostenaco could travel to their place of confinement and identify the warriors.

During May of 1758, Moytoy of Settico and his warriors, mad and surly, just left the Virginia army and headed for home. About twenty of Moytoy's men had lost their horses during the campaign, and the officers rudely refused to replace them. Enroute home, Moytoy's party took the first twenty horses they found. The horses belonged to some Virginia farmers who, naturally, needing their stock, formed a posse and went after the Indians. Locating their camp, they attempted to get the horses back peacefully; but inability to communicate caused a skirmish, with the result that three Indians and one white man were killed. The farmers returned home and sent a local militia company after the Indians. An ambush was set up at a pass through which the Indians would travel and nineteen warriors were killed. The mad Indians began to plunder, burn, and kill in the Yadkin River settlements. Nineteen white scalps, belonging to innocent German farmers, were taken. *(One must remember that Indian custom demanded one white scalp for one dead Indian, no matter whose scalp it was.)*

Virginia officials had also doubled the reward for any French or their allied Indian scalps taken and delivered. The price was thirty pounds per scalp. Some rough border whites took advantage of this bonanza; and, all told, about forty Cherokee warriors lost their scalps and lives in this manner.

In hope of smoothing over some of the bad situations that had developed, The Little Carpenter, second-ranked Chief of the Cherokee Nation, journeyed to Winchester, Virginia, for a conference with Governor Dinwiddie. While in Virginia, The Carpenter and his party were commandeered into the Forbes Camp for scout duty. Not having come for this purpose, The Carpenter and party just up and left. They were pursued, captured, disarmed, and jailed. When news of this humiliation to their Chief reached the Nation, it caused warlike waves of resentment against the Virginians to sweep through the Indian country. When released and allowed to return home, The Carpenter attempted to quiet down the growing war spirit against the British. He was summoned to Charles Town for talks with Governor Lyttleton; and during his absence from Chota, other influences were at work that would bring the Cherokee deep trouble.

FORT LOUDOUN

While The Carpenter was in Charles Town talking with Governor Lyttleton, the Great Mortar, a Creek Chief, arrived in Chota with twenty-three Creek warriors and accompanied by Lantagnac, French representative from Governor Keleric in New Orleans. They were promising plenty of supplies if the Cherokee would leave the English to join the French; and The Mortar was finding plenty of support among many disgruntled Chiefs and warriors. The Mortar and Lantagnac cited many recent incidents which had caused anger between the Cherokee and English. Attention was called to the Fort Prince George incident when Lieutenant Richard Coytmore and Ensign Bell, during a drunken spree, had forced their way into an Indian home in Keowee where they raped two married women whose husbands were away on a hunting trip. Lantagnac cited the requests by Keowee Chiefs for talks which had been refused, and the haughty overbearing attitude of the English officers.

The Great Mortar referred to the widows and sisters mourning the forty warriors killed by the Virginians for their scalps and numerous other incidents of ill treatment by the English. During the council meeting Lantagnac grabbed a war hatchet, struck the painted war pole and cried out, "Who is there that will take the hatchet for the King of France? Let him come

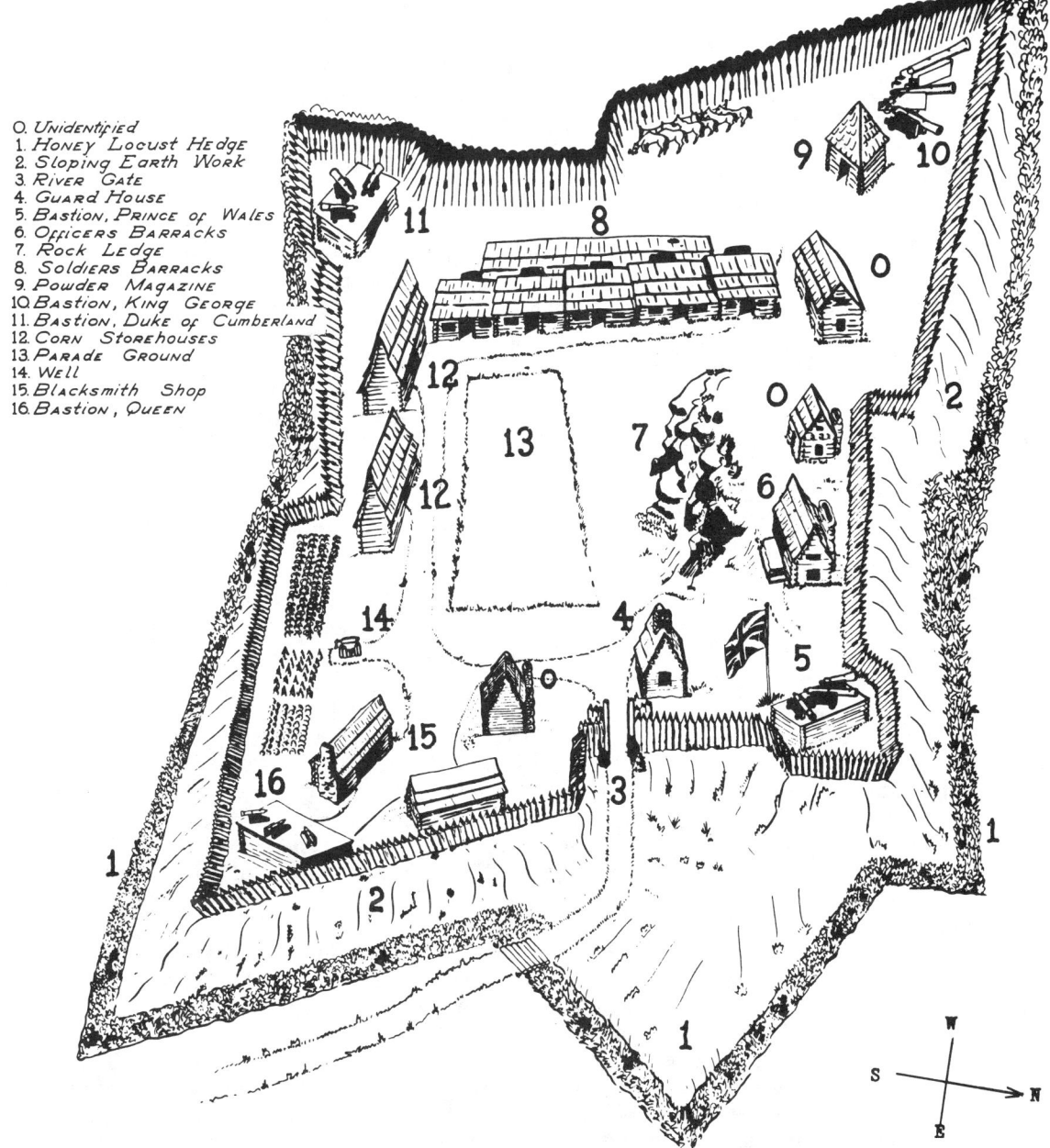

Fort Loudoun on the Little Tennessee River. A Pictorial Restoration based on archaeological investigation, drawn by Garvin M. Colburn for Elsworth Brown, March 11, 1957. *Courtesy Fort Loudoun Association.*

forth." Saloue of Estatoe said, "I will take it." Wauhatchie, Chief of three lower towns, followed Saloue in accepting the hatchet. Most of their warriors were eager to fight. They were mad at English settler encroachers who were moving deeper and deeper into their territory. A great war dance was soon in full swing as the war spirit, aroused by the Frenchman, spread among the warriors. It was not long until war parties from the lower Indian settlements were raiding all along the South Carolina frontiers.

Governor Lyttleton reported to his Council that twenty-two whites had been killed, several others scalped, and that the whole frontier had been terrorized. Most of these raids had been instigated by Lower Town Chiefs. The Middle Towns and Overhill warriors were not greatly involved, but the Governor was determined to teach the Cherokee a lesson. The Council authorized a force of fifteen hundred men for Lyttleton's command.

Oconostota, the Great Cherokee War Chief, heard of the proposed campaign against his people; so he made haste to hold talks with the Governor. Twenty-eight leading Chiefs accompanied him to Charles Town. When the Chiefs arrived at the State House they were ushered into the Council Chamber, where the Governor received them and allowed Oconostota to make his talk:

> Your Excellency is the beloved man; I am come to talk with you. There has been bad doings at the Towns hereabouts but I was not the beginner of them. The path has been a little bad but I am come to make it straight. There has been blood spilled, but I am come to clean it up. I am a warrior but I want no war with the English.

When Oconostota's talk was finished he laid some deer skins on the floor in front of the Governor. Lyttleton replied, "Oconostota, I have permitted you to lay down those skins; but I do not accept them in token of the peace you propose." He then asked the Chief if he came in behalf of the whole Nation. When Oconostota replied that he did, Governor Lyttleton dismissed the Chiefs without further comment. In his report to the State Council the Governor said, "I don't think Oconostota speaks for the Nation. He is only trying to get supplies, ammunition, and presents which the officers at Prince George refused them." The Governor insisted that the expedition against the Cherokee be set in motion.

The chiefs were practically ordered to accompany the English force to Prince George. Oconostota tried to protest, but Governor Lyttleton refused him the right. This was the deepest of insults to a ranking Indian Chief. The English official had broken his word of free and safe passage.

The hard march to Prince George caused grumbling in all quarters. The men marching in the ranks could see no honest reason to fight the Cherokee. Smallpox broke out in camp. Desertions started soon after they left Charles Town. The chiefs were mad and complained all the way. About halfway to Prince George, they were placed under heavy guard. This infuriated them.

When the tired, disgruntled force reached Fort Prince George, Governor Lyttleton had the twenty-eight Chiefs confined in a small cabin inside the fort. There was hardly room for six persons, much less twenty-eight. Twenty-eight prominent Cherokee Chiefs, who had been honored by their own people and courted by the white rulers of two nations were imprisoned by an English Governor who had posed as a friend. It was an act of unadulterated treachery. Following is a quote from a letter written by a South Carolinian about the matter.

> Instead of permitting them (the chiefs) to return home without hurting a hair of their heads, as the Governor had promised in Charles Town, they were close confined in a miserable hut, having permission neither to see friends not even the light of day. . . In whatever light we view the act, it appears to be one of those base and unjustifiable advantages which policy and craft commonly take of the weakness and simplicity of more unfortunate neighbours.

Governor Lyttleton found himself in a mess with an undisciplined army that didn't want to fight, desertions every day, and smallpox all through the camp. He had to find a way out of his plight, so he sent for The Little Carpenter. When the Peace Chief arrived at the fort, Lyttleton told The Carpenter they could have peace under certain conditons:

> First of all you are looking toward the French. They can't help you. They themselves are starving and cannot give you blanket or gun. You have to depend on the English for your needs. Your people have killed twenty-four of ours. I expect you to deliver twenty-four warriors of your nation to be put to death for those your people have murdered.

Little Carpenter frankly told the Governor that it was impossible for him to fulfill this request by himself. He asked that some of the chiefs be released to help him work on the matter. Oconostota and three other Chiefs, Ostenaco, Tiftoe, and Saloue were set free. Two warriors who happened to be present were turned over as hostages for the released Chiefs. The two braves were immediately put in irons; and other warriors who had been hanging around the Fort vicinity fled. Attakullakulla, despondent and worried about the situation, went home to Chota.

Oconostota was mad. He had no intention of surrendering any Cherokee warriors to be shot; but by some means or other he planned to get his brother Chiefs released. In February 1760 he appeared at Fort Prince George. Stopping at the Parade Ground, because of smallpox inside the Fort, he delivered some letters brought from Fort Loudoun to the soldier standing guard. Oconostota also sent his personal request by the soldier, asking for release of the imprisoned Chiefs. Lieutenant Coytmore sent a reply to Oconostota, reminding him of the signed agreement. Oconostota's response was that he had signed no paper, and if the prisoners were not freed he would lead every Cherokee warrior in the Nation against the English.

This demand and threat were ignored; and Oconostota then made up his mind to try another method. He left, but returned to Prince George a few days later. Camped on the river bank across from the Fort, he sent a message to the officers by a squaw known to the Fort guard, asking for talks. Coytmore, accompanied by Lieutenants Bell and Foster and an interpreter came down to the riverside. After a statement or two Oconostota gave a signal and his concealed warriors opened fire on the British party. Coytmore was mortally wounded, and the two Lieutenants were hit but not seriously injured. The Fort party, carrying Coytmore's body, managed to reach the Fort gates which were then closed before Oconostota's warriors could gain entrance. Shots were exchanged, but no serious damage resulted; however, this incident set off a conflict that would have serious results.

Soldiers within the Fort were mad and wanted revenge on the Indians. Ensign Alexander Miln, who had taken over Coytmore's command, tried to restrain the soldiers; and in order to pacify the garrison troops, he gave consent for them to place the captive Chiefs in irons. This was undertaken, but the Indians resisted. Somehow a tomahawk and knife had been secreted in the cabin; and using these weapons, the Indians killed two soldiers and wounded others. The soldiers opened fire on the Chiefs, killing them all.

This wanton murder of so many leading Headmen of the Cherokee spelled doom for Fort Loudoun and all whites living in the Nation. Every white trader who could, fled to the safety of the woods. Bands of warriors began terrorizing the whole frontier. Every pass and trail in and out of the Indian country was guarded. Snipers lay in wait around both Prince George and Loudoun. No soldier dared show himself outside the gate or above Fort walls.

Willenawah, The Carpenter's brother, and young Standing Turkey began the siege of Fort Loudoun in early March 1760. The Carpenter, despairing for his English friends, had taken his family into the woods for safety. Because of his continued friendship for the British he was practically cut off from his own people. The Great Mortar, Creek Chief, was practically running the war against the British.

It has been said that Nancy Ward married Bryant Ward not long after she was chosen as the Cherokee Honored Woman. Some legendary lore hints that it was during the beginning of trouble between the British and Cherokee that Nancy, fearing for Ward's safety, helped arrange for his escape.

Many war parties were ravaging the countryside. One such party was pillaging through the Yadkin River Valley. The Little Carpenter, who was friendly with the Moravians settled at Salem, North Carolina, sent a message of warning to the church community. The message was timely, and families living outside gathered with the townspeople for safety. From the Moravian records comes this story:

> The Warrior Band planning to attack the village of Bethbara had surrounded the small settlement. It happened to be on a Church Day. The bell tolled the hour of worship. The Indians thinking their presence had been discovered withdrew for a conference. They decided to make another attempt during the heavy dark of night. Again they surrounded the town. While waiting the signal for attack they heard the bugler tooting the hour of the night. Certain that their presence had again been discovered and the horn blowing was a warning to those on guard, the Indians left and never bothered the small Moravian settlement.

As the siege of Fort Loudoun continued, food became scarce. Indian women who had married English soldiers were able to smuggle in small quantities of beans and pork to their husbands. For this, Willenawah threatened them with death; but they continued to slip in small amounts hidden in their clothing.

General Jeffrey Amhearst, who had replaced Lord Loudoun as Commander-in-Chief of British Forces in America, had been informed of Loudoun's plight. He sent Colonel Archibald Montgomery with twelve hundred regulars to South Carolina with orders to go to Loudoun's relief. After landing in Charles Town, Montgomery marched toward Fort Prince George. After arriving and setting up camp, he sent squads of men through the lower settlements killing every male found. From there, he set his course toward Loudoun. He met no opposition until he reached a narrow pass called Crows Creek, not many miles from Etchoe. Here a crooked trail ran between the river and an overhanging ridge. The thick growth made it a perfect spot for ambush.

Oconostota, learning of Montgomery's approach by this trail, set up his plan of attack. Montgomery lost about one hundred forty men, killed and wounded in this battle with the Indians. He barely escaped with his own life a number of times. The Indian force, short of ammunition, retreated slowly, keeping up some deadly sniping. Montgomery finally made it to

Etchoe, six miles away. Encumbered with his wounded, the Colonel did not undertake the dangerous march across the hills toward Fort Loudoun. After destroying the town of Etchoe, containing about two hundred dwellings, he headed back in the direction of Fort Prince George. The return trip was rough. Red warriors kept up a continuous sniping attack on the wagons loaded with supplies and wounded men.

The whites inside Loudoun walls heard of Montgomery's coming with hope — they learned of his defeat with despair. Attakullakulla had been able to keep Captain Demere informed of outside events. On one or two occasions he had been able to smuggle some corn and meat inside. These small tidbits of food helped but were not enough, with so many hungry mouths to feed. Faced with starvation inside and death outside, the Fort officers asked the Cherokee for terms of surrender August 7, 1760. The next day they accepted the terms offered by the Chiefs and packed for travel and evacuation. Leaving the Fort on the morning of August 9, they were allowed to take their guns and a small amount of ammunition.

The first day they traveled fifteen miles before making camp. They were accompanied by Oconostota and a sizeable force of warriors; but during the night, all the Indians disappeared. This frightened the officers, who posted guards. Early the next morning, as they were breaking camp, the Indians attacked the soldiers, women, and children. Four officers and twenty-four privates were killed, making a total of twenty-eight dead. The same number of Chiefs had been murdered at Prince George earlier in the year. Several others were wounded and three women were killed before the cease fire order was given.

The remaining captives were dispersed throughout the Nation. No mention is made of Nancy Ward's being called on to use her power as Honored Woman to save any of the captives' lives. It could be that Nancy, as Attakullakulla's close friend, was sort of ignored. Records do indicate some of the men inside the garrison had managed to get away. Isaac Thomas is said to have been one of three men who made such an escape.

Captain John Stuart was taken captive by Onatoy, who by so doing actually saved his life. The Carpenter gave Onatoy his own rifle, coat, and practically all he possessed, except his loin flap, as a ransom for Stuart. He conducted Stuart to Demere's vacant residence inside the Fort until he could arrange for his escape. In the meantime he adopted Stuart as his brother. When things were right The Little Carpenter, aided by family and friends, was able to spirit Stuart out of the Overhill towns and conduct him to Colonel Byrd's camp in Virginia. They arrived there in early December 1760.

TRAGIC AFTERMATH

The Cherokee learned the hard way that their only source of supplies was the English. They liked the French people better, but experience had taught there was little hope in that direction. The Chiefs immediately began making plans to patch up British-Cherokee relations.

Oconostota sent one of the Fort Loudoun captives with a message to Governor Bull, who had replaced Lyttleton as Governor of South Carolina, asking for a Peace Treaty to work out relations between their two nations. Oconostota told of the two thousand Cherokee then meeting in council at Nequasse beneath a raised British flag. His message included the promise that any Englishman could now pass through the Cherokee Nation with safety.

General Jeffrey Amhearst had other plans. News of Fort Loudoun's surrender and the following massacre prompted this remark from the General: "I must own I am ashamed, for I believe it is the first instance of His Majesty's troops having yielded to the Indians." He

Fort Loudoun was gutted by fire soon after its capture by order of Oconostota.

ordered Colonel James Grant to proceed to Charles Town with two thousand troops. Grant's orders were to invade Cherokee country and wipe out the disgrace suffered by His Majesty's troops. Colonel William Byrd of Virginia was ordered to march against the Overhill Towns at the same time.

General Amhearst seemingly disregarded Cherokee participation in the French-Indian war, as well as the possibility that they could easily have joined with the French and destroyed the southern colonies. There were many *ifs* which could have changed the ending of the American story. However, the Cherokee had insulted the British Empire's pride, and for this wrong they must render their pound of flesh.

Colonel Grant arrived in Charles Town sometime in early 1761. Governor Bull placed a provincial regiment, commanded by Colonel Middleton, under Grant's command. Among the officers in Middleton's regiment were William Moultrie and Francis Marion, both of whom would cause the British great trouble a few years hence. Grant's experience with Indian warfare made him wary, so he planned his campaign very carefully.

Colonel Grant learned soon after landing at Charles Town that his march against the Indians was actually unnecessary. The Cherokee were already asking for peace terms. Frontier plantation owners and officers at Prince George saw an opportunity to promote their own gains, however, so they agitated the campaign. Also, Grant had his orders from General Amhearst.

Colonel Grant marched his men to Fort Prince George, arriving there in late May of 1761. Having learned of Grant's projected campaign against his people, The Little Carpenter was waiting at the Fort with a party of Cherokee. Granted a conference, The Carpenter said, "I am, and have been, a friend to the English. For this I have been called an old woman by our warriors. The conduct of my people has filled me with shame but I would interpose in their behalf and bring about peace." The Carpenter's words fell on deaf ears. Grant refused to discuss the situation until the Cherokee had been chastised for the destruction of Fort Loudoun.

The British force left Prince George and headed for the Valley and Middle Towns. Two days of hard travel brought Grant to Etchoe Pass near where Oconostota had earlier defeated Montgomery's force. Grant was determined his command would not suffer a similar defeat.

Hopeful for another victory over the British, Oconostota had placed his warriors in strategic ambush cover along the trail; but Grant had anticipated just such a surprise attack, and planned accordingly. He sent a company of his Catawba Indian allies and some experienced white woodsmen, dressed as Indians, ahead of his main force. Oconostota had hoped to hold his fire until the main English force was in range; but the Catawbas made an early flanking charge before Grant's main force arrived. Oconostota's warriors sounded their battle cry and with war whoops began the battle. Grant was able to outmaneuver Oconostota during this four hour engagement. Finally the Cherokee ammunititon gave out and they had to withdraw. Lack of powder and shot, rather than Grant's strength, was the contributing factor in Oconostota's defeat. Cherokee dependence on white man's supplies had become an important element in their existence and survival.

Grant moved his force on to Etchoe (located near present Franklin, North Carolina). Here he took over the Town House for his wounded men. Grant's journal had this entry for June 13, 1761:

> We halted (at Etchoe). Corn about the town was destroyed, parties were sent out to burn the scattered houses, pull up beans, peas and corn, and to demolish everything eatable in the country. Our Indian Scouts, with one of our parties, destroyed the towns of Neowee and Kanuga. A scout of our Indians killed a Cherokee and wounded another at Ayore. A miserable old squaw from Tasso was brought in and put to death in the Indian Camp by the Catawbas.

Leaving the disabled men under guard, Grant and his men made a night march across the mountains to the main settlements of the Middle Towns. The pass was so narrow and dangerous that the men had to travel single file. Fifty warriors with bows and arrows could have stopped them. This was the first time on record that the Middle Towns had ever been invaded by an enemy force. Grant's report stated that fifteen towns were destroyed, fifteen hundred acres of crops cut down, and five thousand Cherokee were driven into the mountains to starve.

A letter written by Lieutenant Francis Marion and taken from *Life of General Francis Marion* by P. Horry is quoted:

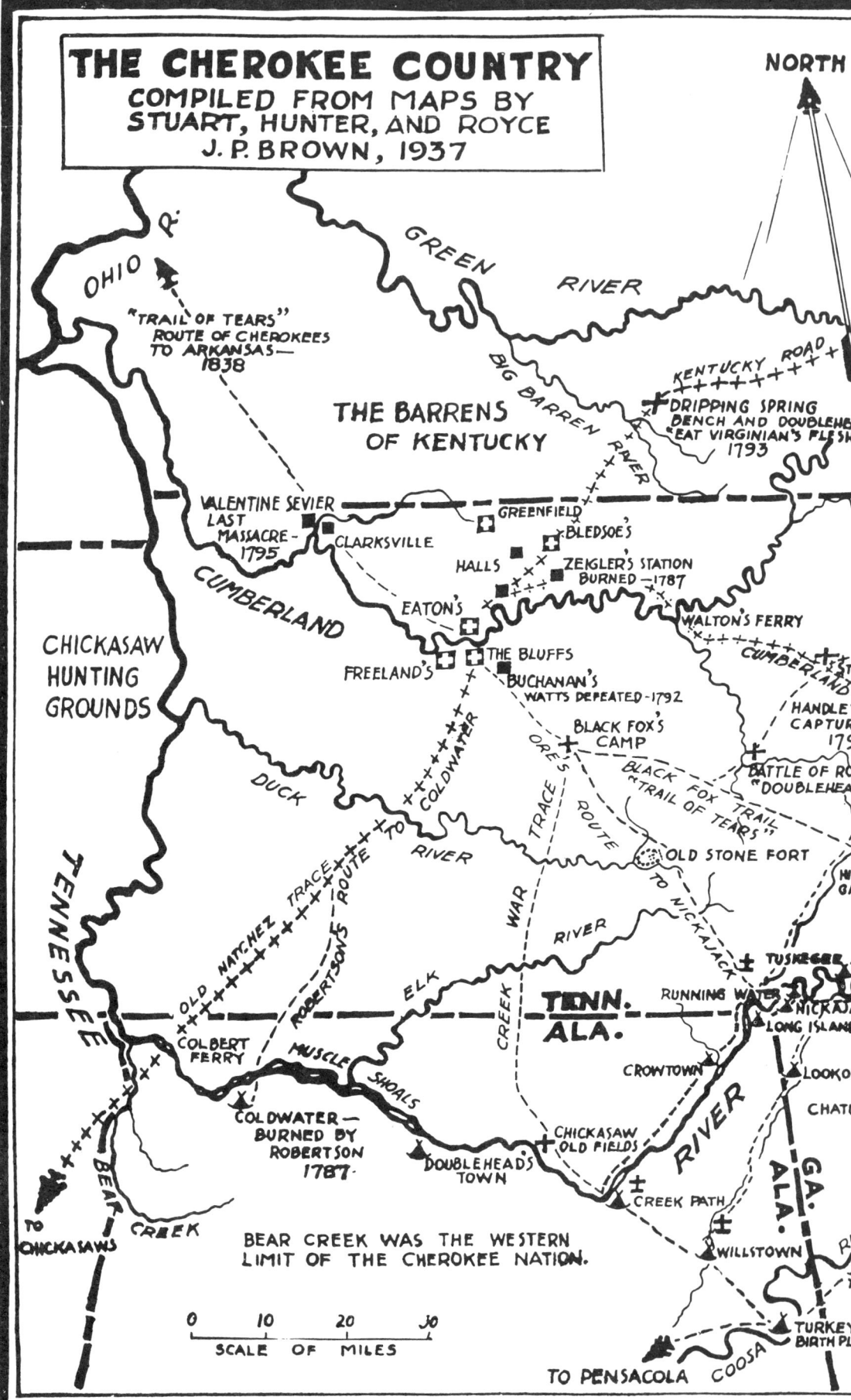

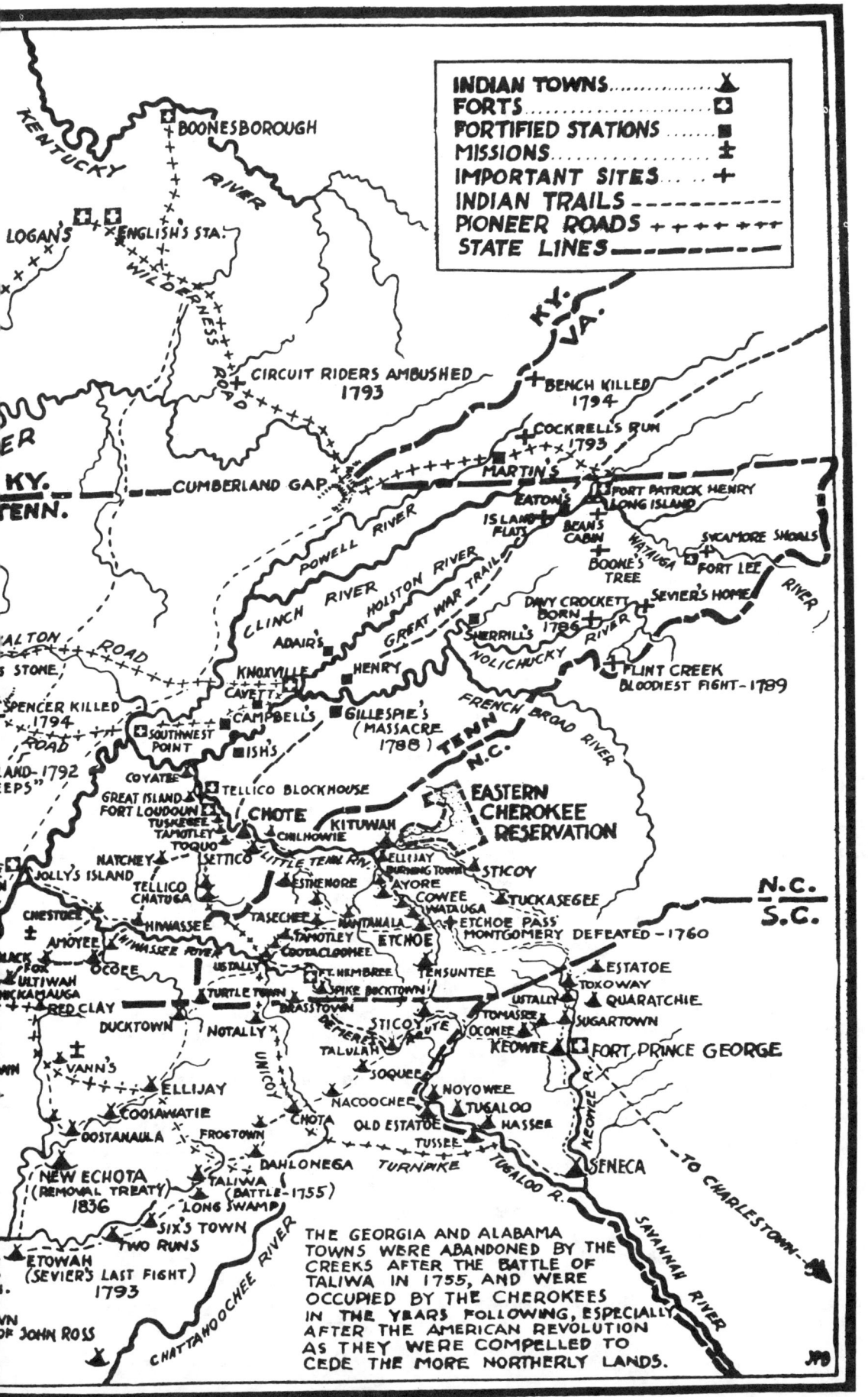

We proceeded, by Colonel Grant's orders, to burn the Indian cabins. Some of the men seemed to enjoy this cruel work, laughing heartily at the curling flames, but to me it appeared a shocking sight. Poor creatures, thought I, we surely need not grudge you such miserable habitations. But when we came, according to orders, to cut down the fields of corn, I could scarcely refrain from tears. Who, without grief, could see the stately stalks with broad green leaves and tasseled tops, the staff of life sink under our swords with all their precious load, to wither and rot untasted in their mourning field.

I saw everywhere around, the footsteps of little Indian children, where they had lately played under the shade of their rustling corn. When we are gone, thought I, they will return, and peeping through the weeds with tearful eyes, will mark the ghastly ruin where they had so often played. "Who did this?" they will ask their mothers, and the reply will be: "The white people did it — the Christians did it."

Thus for cursed mammon's sake, the followers of Christ have sowed the selfish tares of hate in the bosom of even pagan children.

Grant led his army back to Fort Prince George, arriving there in mid July 1761. He immediately sent a message to leading Cherokee Chiefs to come to the Fort for talks. The Little Carpenter, Ostenaco, The Raven of Chota, Ole Caesar of Hiwassee, and fifteen other Chiefs left for the conference with Grant.

Nancy Ward's first six years as a member of the Cherokee State Council must have been quite an experience for the young unseasoned Chieftainess. She must have heard talks concerning the bloody incidents in Virginia, listened to the arguments favoring alliance with the French, and experienced the tragedies of Grant's destruction of the Middle Towns when the Overhill Towns were crowded with refugees seeking safety. The Cherokee War Chiefs were experiencing first hand the consequence of white man's superior numbers, devastating fire power, and unity of purpose. Somber thoughts must have passed through Nancy Ward's mind as she watched the Head Chiefs of the Nation leave for this treaty-meet demanded by Grant.

When the Chiefs arrived at Fort Prince George, Grant received them in a special bower erected for the occasion. The terms for the peace treaty were read and interpreted for the Chiefs, who agreed to all the conditions except one. This particular item demanded that four Cherokee warriors be delivered to Grant to be executed in front of his men as an atonement for the destruction of Fort Loudoun, or that four green Cherokee scalps be brought to him within twelve days.

The Little Carpenter was appalled at this demand and replied, "I do not have the authority to fulfill such a condition." He requested permission to go to Charles Town and lay the matter before Governor Bull. The request was granted.

When The Carpenter and his party arrived at Charles Town they were well received by the Governor. The whole mess, the Virginia incidents, the massacre of the twenty-eight chiefs, Montgomery's defeat, the fall of Fort Loudoun, and Grant's campaign had been needless. Governor Bull realized this and made congenial gestures to bring about friendly relationships. Governor Bull's greeting to the Cherokee Party was thus recorded:

> Attakullakulla, I am glad to see you. As you have always been a good friend to the English, I take you by the hand, and not only you but those with you, as a pledge of their security while under my protection. Colonel Grant has acquainted me that you have applied for peace. I am now met with my beloved men to hear what you have to say, and my ears are open for that purpose.

After lighting his pipe and passing it to the Governor and Council members, The Carpenter presented a string of wampum to the Governor and replied, "You live at the waterside and are in light. We are in darkness, but hope that all will yet be clear with us. I have been constantly going about doing good, and though I am tired yet am come to see what can be done for my people, who are in great distress." He ended with, "I hope, as we all live in one land, we shall live as one people."

Governor Bull left out the clause demanding the execution of four braves and admonished them to be faithful and punctual in the performance of the other articles. By the treaty terms, all English prisoners held by the Cherokee were to be released. Likewise, all Cherokee prisoners held by the British were to be freed. The formal signing of the Peace Treaty was accomplished December 16, 1761. The Cherokee-English war thus ended — a war forced on the Cherokee by unwarranted actions of the British and the haughty attitude of their political and military officials.

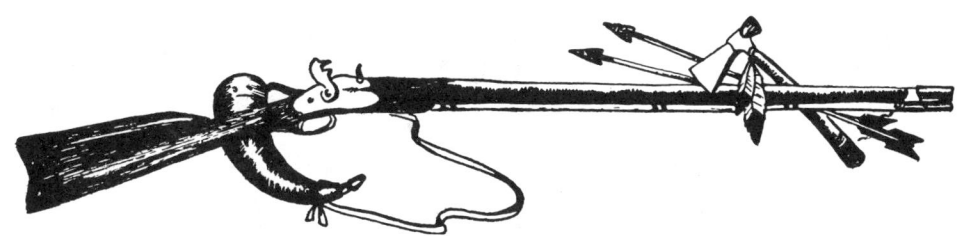

TROUBLES...SURPRISES...TREATIES

General Amhearst had ordered Colonel Richard Byrd to march his Virginia command toward Fort Loudoun and against the Overhill Cherokee at the same time he had instructed Colonel James Grant to move against the Lower and Middle Towns from Fort Prince George. Colonel Byrd gave one excuse after another as to why he didn't march as ordered.

The Little Carpenter had approached Grant at Fort Prince George May 27, 1761, asking for peace talks; but Grant refused any discussions until he had chastised the Cherokee for destroying Fort Loudoun. The Carpenter set out immediately for Colonel Byrd's camp in Virginia, arriving there July 18. Byrd told the Chief he would have to make his peace arrangements with Colonel Grant before he could help.

From the beginning, Colonel Byrd had little heart for the campaign. He and The Carpenter were friends of several years standing. During the year 1756, Colonel Byrd was a member of an English Commission delegated to hold talks with the Cherokee for the purpose of persuading them to join the English against the French. The Treaty was held on the Broad River in North Carolina. During the meet, Cherokee warriors, who accompanied their Chiefs, received word that some of their brother warriors had been killed up north by British soldiers. Angered, these braves were ready to kill any Englishmen to get even. The Commissioners were in danger. The Carpenter, aided by Chief Saloue, managed to get the English Commissioners to a cabin where they could barricade themselves until the angry warriors were quieted.

Rather than march against the Cherokee and his friend The Little Carpenter, Colonel Byrd resigned his command and went home. Lieutenant Colonel Adam Stephen, who had succeeded Byrd, soon broke camp and marched toward Long Island. Major Andrew Lewis and his company had been sent ahead to cut a road, and also to start construction on a fort near the upper end of Long Island. After marching for several days, Stephen's force arrived at the fort location and aided Lewis in completing the structure. It was occupied in the middle of November, 1761, and named Fort Robinson. Shortly after its completion, Willinaw, Little Carpenter's brother, and Standing Turkey, accompanied by about four hundred Cherokee warriors, arrived to arrange the Peace Treaty with the Virginians. The Little Carpenter, busy with the South Carolina sessions, had sent instructions by Willinaw.

After the treaty sessions were completed, Standing Turkey asked Colonel Stephen to send a British representative to the nation as an expression of English sincerity in keeping their promises of peace with the Cherokee. Lieutenant Henry Timberlake and Sergeant Thomas Sumpter volunteered to make the trip. Timberlake, Sumpter, and John McCormack (interpreter) decided to make the trip by dugout canoe rather than go with the Cherokee party on the overland trail. The river trip almost turned into a disaster.

Timberlake and his party finally arrived in the Overhills December 20, 1761. The overland Cherokee party had returned several days earlier. The English party was greeted at Tomotley by Chief Ostenaco, who invited Timberlake to be his house guest during his stay. Sumpter and McCormack received similar invitations from other town officials.

Early during Timberlake's stay, he was invited to attend a State Council Meet at Chota to read and discuss the peace terms recently signed at Fort Robinson. Later he was invited to attend a gala event at Great Tellico. This was the town where much of the Cherokee trouble with the British had originated.

Timberlake's *Memoirs* is largely an account of his five-month stay in the Overhill country. His descriptions of the people, ceremonials both civil and religious, dances, building structures, variety of trees, wild animals, method of fishing, cooking, foods, and status of women have been a valuable source of information about the Cherokee people during the middle of the 18th century. Emmet Starr, Cherokee historian, says that Timberlake's consortium with a Cherokee maiden left a son named Richard Timberlake in the nation.

Richard's son, Levi Timberlake, married a great granddaughter of Nancy Ward. Allison Timberlake, their son, married Margaret Lavinia Rogers, paternal aunt of Will Rogers. Many prominent descendants of this family now live in Oklahoma.

Ostenaco, Timberlake's host, accompanied Timberlake back to Virginia. While visiting Governor Fauquier at Williamsburg, Ostenaco prevailed upon the Governor to let him visit England. Timberlake, Sumpter, William Shorey (interpreter), and two warriors made up the party for the voyage. The Chief made a farewell talk to his guards who had accompanied him to Williamsburg. The occasion is described by Thomas Jefferson, then a student at William and Mary College:

> I know much of the great Ostenaco, the warrior and orator of the Cherokee. He was always the guest of my father on his way to and from Williamsburg. I was in his camp when he made his farewell oration to his people the evening before he departed for England. The moon was in full splendor, and to it he seemed to address himself in his prayers for his own safety on the voyage and that of his people during his absence. His sounding voice, distinct articulation, animated action, and the solemn silence of his people at their several fires, filled me with awe and veneration, although I did not understand a word he uttered.

A sketch of Ostenaco, also known as Outacite, made by the court artist, Sir Joshua Reynolds, while the Chief was visiting London in company with Lieutenant Henry Timberlake in 1762.

William Shorey, Ostenaco's interpreter, died at sea, and since there was no interpreter during the Chief's audience with King George II, they could converse only with sign language. He made a speech concluding with the statement, "I shall tell my people all that I have seen in England." When Ostenaco returned to Charles Town he repeated his entire address to Governor Bull who sent a translated copy to the King. A letter from John Stuart also informed British officials that Ostenaco's amazing accounts of His Majesty's power and grandeur had greatly enhanced England's standing in the Nation.

Another surprising visitor came to the Overhill country during this decade. Following is a quote from *Springplace, Moravian Mission Cherokee Nation* by Muriel H. Wright:

> In 1764 John (Jack) Ward, a native of Ireland, leaving the ship on which he had sailed to America, set out for the Cherokee country. Arriving at Echota (Chota which is near Fort Loudoun, Tennessee) he learned that his father Bryant Ward, for whom he was seeking, had separated from his Cherokee wife, Nancy Ward, and no longer lived in the Nation.
>
> Brian Ward had served in the British Army during the Colonial Wars in America. He was a descendant of the Irish Nobility and was a relative of an officer in the British Army, by the name of Ward. When his military service ended, his wife having died in Ireland, Brian Ward became a trader among the Cherokee. Under a tribal law instituted at an early date, no white man could remain permanently in the

Cherokee country and have the protection of the Cherokee Chiefs unless he married into the tribe and made his home in the tribal domain.

John Ward found his stepmother, Nancy Ward, the most influential woman among her people, the Cherokee. She was wealthy in her own right and was highly respected, both by them and the Americans, in her position as the Ghigau or Beloved Woman of her nation.

John Ward remained in the Cherokee Country and married Catherine McDaniel, best know in her family as *Katie*. She was the 17-year-old daughter of a Scotchman named McDaniel and his fullblooded Cherokee wife called *Granny Hopper*. John and Katie Ward had eight children: James, George, Samuel, Charles, Bryant, Betsy, Susie and Nancy Lucy. Many prominent American families can trace their heritage back to this family.

The year 1768 became known as the year of treaties. Coastal settlers began moving into Cherokee country along the foothills of the mountains. They were building cabins and making improvements on their squatter claims near Indian towns. In efforts to appease the Indians and at the same time halt the constant encroachment of the whites on the red men's soil, King George III set up a definite line by proclamation in 1763. This line ran along the crest of the Blue Ridge Mountain range, from Georgia to New Hampshire. This was not a popular decree. It made land companies, small farmers, ambitious squatters, and a host of newcomers mad. The proclamation also strictly stated that no private person could purchase land from the Indians or settle beyond the proclamation line. The main purpose of the decree was to assure the Indians that their hunting grounds belonged to them.

Two Indian superintendents were appointed by the King to supervise and protect Indian rights from north to south. This was a grand gesture, but like all other laws, decrees, and rules, it only partially worked. Sir William Johnson was placed in charge of Indian affairs in the territory north of the Ohio. Captain John Stuart, Attakullakulla's friend, was appointed as superintendent to supervise all the tribes south of the Ohio River. Stuart was kept busy trying to appease the Indians for constant encroachment on their southern lands and making what efforts he could to stop further squatter settlements. American frontiersmen were also casting hungry, greedy looks at the lush valleys lying beyond the Appalachian Mountains. They would soon be moving in that direction.

John Stuart had to work out many treaties during the 1760 decade to keep peace. Many squatters who had settled beyond the proclamation line refused to move. Stuart had to work out treaties to legalize these claims. The first line was run from Reedy River in South Carolina, by way of Tryon Mountain, to the Chiswell Mine (Fort Chiswell) in Virginia. The Hard Labor Treaty of 1768 was an extension of the Tryon Mountain line. In 1770, the Lockaber Treaty was signed by the Cherokee. During the year 1771, this line was changed to follow the Kentucky River. Piece by piece, the Cherokee land was being gobbled by English, land companies, frontier families, and squatters. There seemed to be no end to white man's thirst for Indian land.

Indians viewed with apprehension each new cabin.

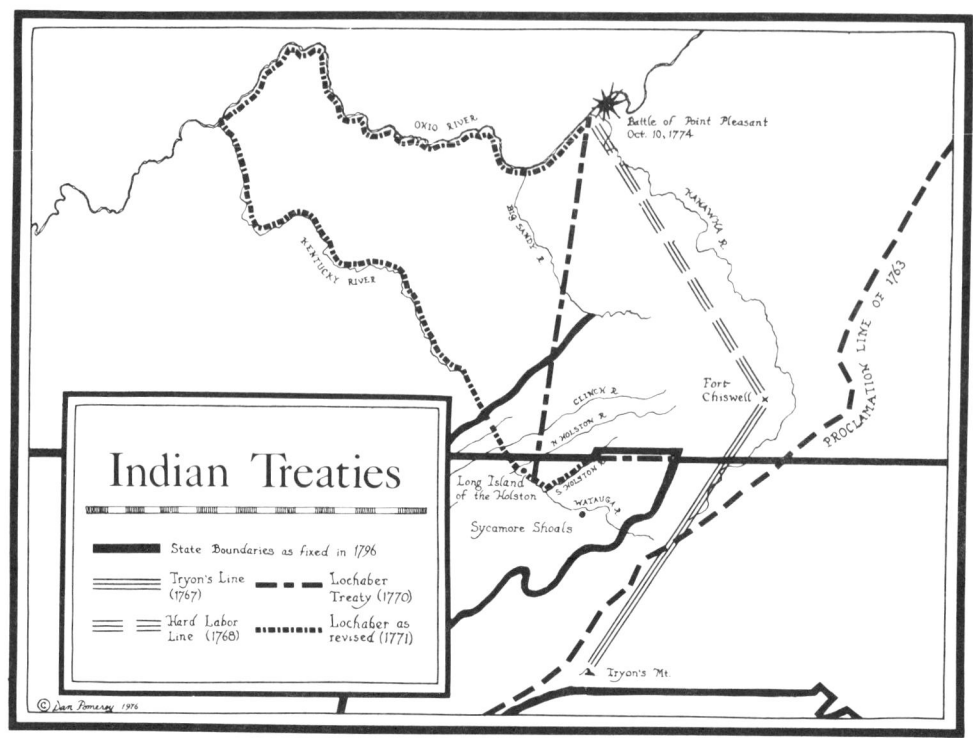

Illustration map indicates treaty lines of the 1760s including the King's Proclamation line of 1763.
Line drawing by Dan Pomeroy courtesy The Wataugans *by Max Dixon.*

Corn was the Cherokee's chief produce and their main dependence. Here Mrs. Mollie Sequoyah is shown in the *Oconaluftee Village* grinding corn in a large wooden mortar, using the heavy wood pestle to pound the grains into meal. *Oconaluftee Village* has been re-created to show lifestyles and culture of Cherokee people 200 years ago.

The Council House is the center of political and religious life of the Cherokee. It is a seven-sided building, each side representing one of the seven clans. The seats are raised one above the other for benefit of clan members. The sacred altar fire is in a cleared area in the center and the principal Chief's seat occupies the central place back of the Sacred Fire.

THE INDIAN AND HIS LAND
From Colonialism into Nationalism

The decline of Indian culture and the loss of his land began the day Columbus accidentally discovered the wooded shores of the New World. He was actually searching for a shorter route to India and thought he had reached that country; so Columbus called the natives Indios (Indians). His discovery of their homeland ignited a bloody struggle between European nations that would eventually spell disaster to the aborigines of the Americas and their way of life.

When those first Spanish ships touched American shores, the natives greeted the strange white visitors with gifts and generous hospitality. The Spaniards considered this friendly welcome and generosity a sign of weakness. Columbus later sailed to the shores of Cuba, where he planted the flag of Spain and claimed all the lands in the name of the king. This event signaled the beginning of the end for the red man's tribal domain.

News of the New World's discovery spread throughout the European countries and triggered a long period of bloody struggle for its colonial control and supremacy. Spain, France, England, Holland and others began moving toward this new Utopia with grasping hands. The Spanish continued their thrust of conquest into Florida and all lands touching the Gulf of Mexico. The French planted their flag in Canada and moved down the Mississippi Basin. England and Holland planted colonies along the Atlantic seaboard.

Decades passed, with the surge of newly arriving immigrants increasing yearly. As settlements became crowded, newcomers pushed inland looking for unclaimed land. They saw vast stretches of wilderness, seemingly uninhabited except for scattered tribal towns and villages of ignorant savages who had no recorded claim or title to the land. Confronted with no legal barriers, Colonial Europeans moved on to Indian Territory one way or another. They used just about every possible ruse and method of deceit to take Indian land. The natives were too inexperienced and too few in number to halt the sheer force of the advancing hordes. An old Indian saying is, "It was not the white man's armies nor governments that finally beat us. It was the constant inrush of settlers. Get rid of one pioneer family and ten more took their place."

Common laws, customs, and accepted practices brought by immigrants from Europe and transplanted in the New Country were the basis of many bloody conflicts that developed between white men and red men. The laws of most European governments stipulated that individuals could obtain deeds, titles, or charters, which gave legalized rights of property, and could be recorded to private ownership to be bought or sold at will. The Colonists merely moved their laws, courts, land deed practices, and way of life to America, establishing their European type of government in the world of the Indian and expecting him to accept without too much struggle. To the white man, land was a commodity to live from — an object of trade and barter. The vast wilderness offered good farming space when cleared of trees which were used to build cabins, and the forests were filled with wild game offering meat for the table and pelts which would bring fancy prices in Europe; and it all seemed free for the taking.

White settlers could not or would not understand Indian viewpoints or age-old traditions. European ways of life, paper writing and law courts were strange and confusing to the red people. They were unable to cope with the situation since they were in no way prepared to compete in the white man's world. The Indian had no formal or written language when the white man first entered his world. There were no written deeds, no Indian surveyors to determine claim boundaries, no register of deeds office to record land titles, no written constitution, and no statute of laws or courts of justice to protect their rights. It was inevitable that these two conflicting ideologies and cultures would clash.

One of the amazing facts of American-Indian history is that so many aborigine societies managed to endure as independent tribal entities so late into the latter part of the 19th century, when so many efforts, moral and immoral, legal and illegal, were made to destroy their tribal unity. A moral and legal right for taking the Indian lands has never been satisfactorily determined. Quite often, public officials explain to us what the moral and legal laws are, or should be. Actions and practices of mankind, in high and low places, tell us what the laws really are.

The unrecorded Indian land claims furnished open doors to unscrupulous speculators and uncaring, fraudulent officials, for raping American tribes of their natural heritage and resources. Treatment of native tribal societies epitomizes the progressive strides of American civilization of which Indians were victims. Spaniards viewed the Indians as a curiosity who posed no serious threat. Colonists saw them as ignorant savages to be exploited. Frontier settlers regarded the Indians as an uncivilized enemy to be destroyed or pushed out of the way.

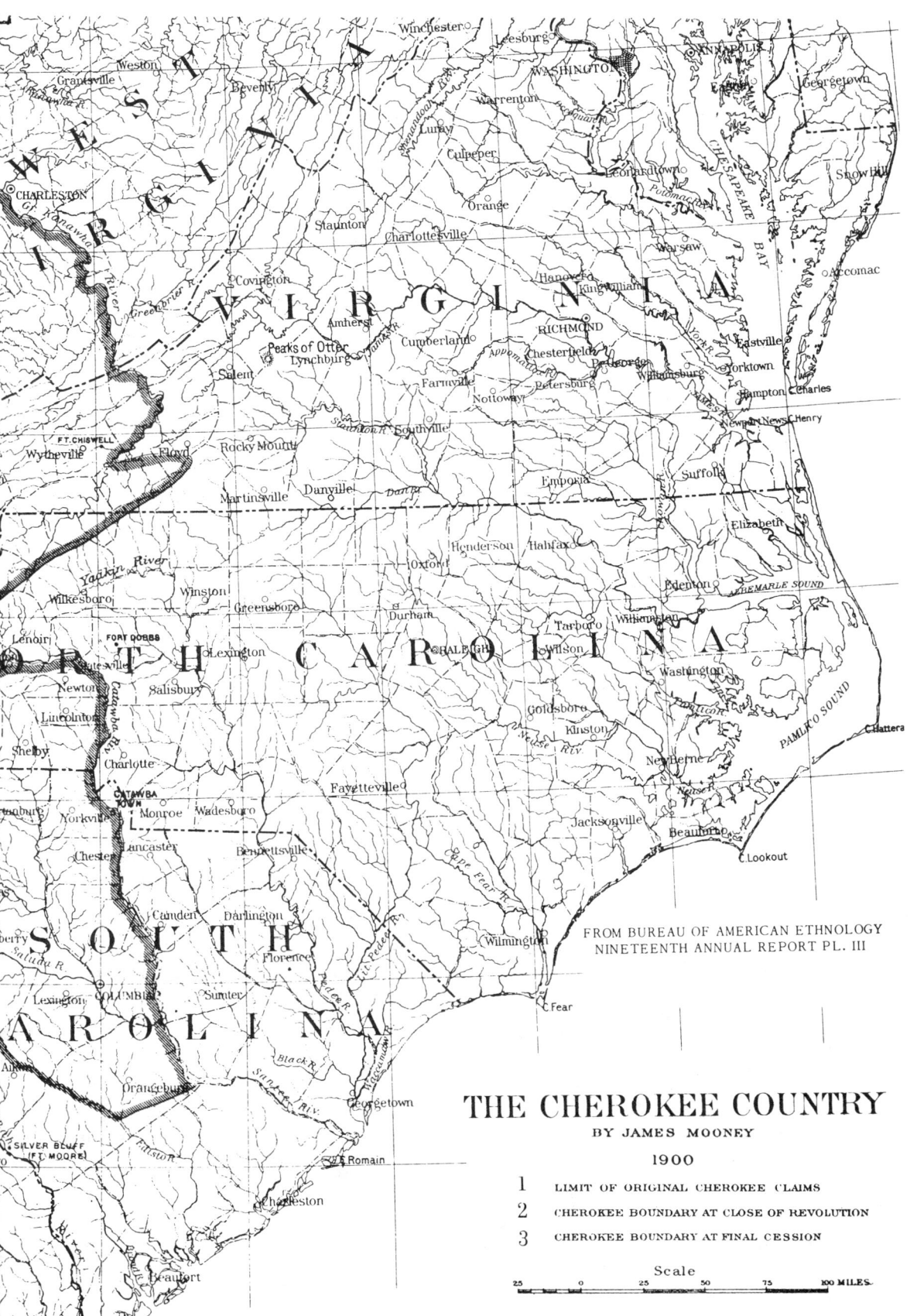

From prehistoric times on through the 18th and much of the 19th centuries, Indian ownership of land stemmed from ancestral tradition and custom. They lived with the land, and their lives were centered within the natural and spiritual world. For centuries they had experienced and survived with equanimity two worlds, one natural and the other human, in an environment that was in balance with man's being. Their souls, minds, bodies, and strength were adjusted to the demands of their environment. An Indian could see beauty and design in the natural world. At the same time he excelled in the joy of living and was content with his way of life.

All tribal Indian societies, especially those east of the Mississippi River, believed the lands were given to them by the Great Spirit and could not be sold, bartered, or appropriated to individual ownership. Land was given them to live on as custodians, to hunt, fish, and farm for food. Nothing could be sold or traded except those things which could be moved from place to place. Indians believed that land was placed here to be used by those living, shared with all living creatures, and held in trust for generations yet to come.

Natives were willing to share the use of the land with their white brothers; thus, even though they received goods and supplies for its use, their early treaty-trade agreements with the whites were based on ancient Indian thinking and tradition. Tribal ownership of land by the whole society had come down through many generations, from early aborigine permanent settlements through colonialism into nationalism. They did not consider the treaty deals final and permanent. Indians were not equipped government-wise, penny-wise, or experience-wise to deal with the cunning shrewdness of land-hungry greedy colonists. When the Indians discovered how their heritage was being taken from them, it was too late and the whites had become too numerous to stop the big land grabs. Indians were powerless to combat the legal methods employed by white men. They became controlled by the laws and courts established in the New World by European colonists — courts in which the red man had no easy redress for his grievances. Indian evidence was not permitted in white man's early legal institutions.

One of the tragedies of American progress has been the misery of displaced Indian societies, overcome by aggressive forces whose desire was to own and dominate. During the decade following the Revolutionary War, the United States Congress made ineffectual efforts to handle Indian affairs. Congressional representatives were elected by the Thirteen States, each of whom insisted that their individual state rights came first and could not be infringed upon. Land poor New England states wanted Virginia, North Carolina, and Georgia to cede their vast land claims to Congress for the common good to pay the national war debt. North Carolina was determined to use Cherokee lands to pay off her own war debts. Virginia, the two Carolinas, and Georgia considered Cherokee land as spoils of war after England was defeated.

Various elements contributed to the course followed and actions taken by the United States in dealing with the Indian and his land. The Cherokee became one of the first Indian societies of America to experience the thrust of new United States Government officials in handling Indian affairs. Haphazard policies used during those early years by State and Federal authorities crystallized into a sort of unofficial pattern, later followed in dealing with other tribal societies in America.

During the two hundred years of our country's existence, nearly all Indian tribes have been physically subdued and shattered, the remnants pushed into unproductive, restricted reservations. They have been forced to outwardly assume white man's civilization in order to survive. The Cherokee attitude toward tribal ownership was expressed in a resolution adopted in October 1838 by the Last Council Meeting held on their native homeland soil before the first company started on the tragic *Trail of Tears*.

> The title of the Cherokee people to their lands is the most ancient, pure, and absolute known to man; its date is beyond the reach of human record; its validity confirmed by possession and enjoyment antecedent to all pretense of claim by any portion of the human race.
>
> The free consent of the Cherokee people is indispensable to a valid transfer of the Cherokee title. The Cherokee people have neither by themselves nor their representatives given such consent. It follows that the original title and ownership of said lands still rests in the Cherokee Nation, unimpaired and absolute. The Cherokee people have existed as a distinct national community for a period extending into antiquity beyond the dates and records and memory of man. These attributes have never been relinquished by the Cherokee people, and cannot be dissolved by the expulsion of the Nation from its own territory by the power of the United States Government.

THE WATAUGA PEOPLE

Our narrative up to now has been mainly concerned with the Cherokee's relationship with the colonists of Virginia, the two Carolinas, and Georgia. The Long Hunter invasion of the Upper East Tennessee territory during the 1760s introduced new dimensions into the story, along with several events that were part of the Revolutionary War. This part of our story also formally brings Nancy Ward and Dragging Canoe onto the national scene.

Daniel Boone and scores of hunters began exploring the Overmountain country along the Holston, Watauga, and Clinch Rivers about 1760, according to records and the *Daniel Boone Bar Tree*. These hunter-explorers would stay away from home months at a time, hence the name *Long Hunter*. They would return to the settlements, their pack horses laden with animal pelts, telling glowing tales of a land across the mountains teeming with wild game, uninhabited wilderness watered by creeks and rivers, towering mountains forested with virgin timber, land as rich as manure, and no tax collectors banging on the door. As these stories passed from settlement to settlement, the Overmountain country became a magnet, pulling people across the invisible boundary lines of 1763 decreed by the King and His Royal Governors.

William Bean, an earlier hunting associate of Boone, left his Virginia home and returned to the Watauga River basin during 1768. Locating a desirable site near the mouth of a stream, which he named *Boone's Creek*, he cleared a patch of land and built a cabin before returning home. In the spring of 1769, Bean moved his family into the lower Watauga River area. The Beans were soon followed by John and George Russell, brothers of Mrs. Bean. Other Virginia neighbors, excited by the bold venture, were soon staking claims and building cabins near the Beans. The downstream Watauga settlement gradually became a sizeable community.

James Robertson, from North Carolina, decided to explore the transmountain country people were talking about. He followed Boone's trail through the Yadkin River country, crossed mountain range at Boone's Gap, followed the old Indian Trail past site of Zionville, Trade, on down Roan Creek, into the valley of the Watauga (Sycamore Shoals, Elizabethton, Tennessee). There he found the Old Fields and ancient Indian village sites long ago cleared of virgin trees. Robertson cleared enough land to plant a small patch of corn, then built a cabin and corn crib before leaving for home. It is said that about sixteen families returned with Robertson to the Overmountain country in 1771. This large number of emigrants passing through North Carolina settlements was bound to excite active curiosity and interest in the lands that lay beyond the mountains.

To the northeast of the Watauga settlement, another group was putting down stakes. Evan Shelby and son Isaac had made arrangements to purchase part of the Granville grant north of the Holston. They built a cabin, store, and stockade; moved the family there; and called it Sappling Grove (now Bristol, Tennessee-Virginia). The Shelby settlement, although not part of Watauga, played an important role in the Overmountain story.

Southwest of the Watauga settlement another element was added to the western drama. Jacob Brown, Indian trader, blacksmith, and farmer, purchased squatter rights from one John Ryan, who had located on the Nolichucky River. Brown either built a cabin or used an empty log structure left by Ryan, and soon had a crude blacksmith shop and storehouse raised on the north banks of the Nolichucky River. It was not very long until Cherokee hunters discovered Brown's blacksmith, gun repair shop, and supply store, which soon became a sort of Indian hunter hangout. Here they could meet, trade their pelts, have their guns mended, and obtain powder and lead and needed supplies in the middle of their hunting grounds.

The Watauga and Nolichucky settlements were both more than fifty miles beyond the King's proclamation line of 1763. They were not within the jurisdiction of either Virginia or North Carolina. The Donelson line survey that had been required by the Lochaber Treaty gave Alexander Cameron, Deputy British Superintendent to the Cherokee, all the excuse he needed. He sent a warning to the new settlements to move off the Indian land and relinquish all claims. From North Carolina's Colonial Records comes this statement by Brown in his 1776 petition for his legal claim to the Nolichucky purchase:

> Some time after a line being run and a Proclamation Issued by his Britanic Majesty's Superintendent of Indian affairs requiring all persons who had made settlement beyond the said line to relinquish them, Your Petitioner altho' much sollicited by the Indians of the Cherokee Nation to remain in his settlement yet did remove himself with much trouble and disadvantage to Wattagaw, where he remained until the Chief of the said Nation by very pressing Intreaty and great Incouragement prevailed on him your Petitioner to return to his former settlement whither a Considerable Body of Indians of the aforesaid Nation Escorted your Petitioner and assisted in removing his Effects.

The warning from Cameron created a critical situation for the Watauguans. Decisions had to be made, and fast. Should they leave or fight? They looked at their new cabin homes, their cleared crop lands, and made their decision. They would stay. The Watauguans began to use delaying tactics, stalling for time. Oconostota wrote to Superintendent Stuart April 26, 1772, giving this account:

> A few days ago Jamie Branham (Overhill Trader) was among them (The Watauguans) to see how many Plantations they had, which were about Seventy. They asked him if our Brother, Mr. Cameron, was not a mad man or a fool that he did not send them word before they had Planted; that they had now planted their crops and would not move off till they had got them in.

The Watauguans talked, planned, and discussed. They could not legally buy the land, and finally it was decided to see if they could finesse a lease agreement with the Chiefs. In this way the enemy would become their landlord. Jacob Brown is credited by some writers with suggesting the lease plan.

James Robertson and John Bean were delegated to visit the Cherokee towns and hold talks about a lease arrangement. The two Watauguans were received by the Indians in a friendly manner and invited to meet with the Tribal Council for talks. A white trader, familiar with the Cherokee language, had to translate for both parties. Robertson soon learned that the Chiefs were divided in their opinions concerning the lease. He sought out those who were favorable and presented gifts along with his most persuasive talks through the interpreter. When the matter was voted on in the Council, the majority were in favor of

James Robertson and John Bean are delegated to visit the Cherokee Council at Chota in an attempt to arrange a lease agreement. (Scene from an outdoor production of *The Overmountain Men* by Pat Alderman.)

granting the lease. Even Henry Stuart, English Deputy Indian Superintendent, had been persuaded. This surprised Alexander Cameron who vigorously opposed the arrangement, as did many of the younger Chiefs.

Attakullakulla, "The Little Carpenter," was delegated to go to Watauga and work out the details of the lease arrangement. Likely a resident trader went along as interpreter. Before leaving Chota, The Carpenter sent Stuart this message:

> Father, I will eat and drink with my white brothers, and will expect friendship and

good usage from them. It is but a little spot of ground they ask, and I am willing that your people should live upon it. I pity the white people, but they do not pity me... The Great Being above is very good, and provides for everybody... He gave us this land, but the white people seem to want to drive us from it.

The Little Carpenter went to Watauga and worked out the details of the lease and friendship pact. The agreement was a ten-year permit, which made the Cherokee landlords of the Wataugans during the tenure of the treaty. The Cherokee were to receive the equivalent of a thousand or more dollars in trade goods, guns, powder, and lead. Jacob Brown made similar arrangements with the Indians for his Nolichucky land. Moses Fisk, an early writer, says:

Jacob Brown... settled on Nolichucky River, a step nearer the scalpers. There he kept a little supply of goods suited to their taste and conveniency, in order to maintain a traffic with them to advantage. And by this means ingratiating himself into their favor, he soon courted them to a treaty in which he contracted for the lands on the Nolachucky [sic] as had been done on the Watauga.

Paul Fink, historian, has said that Brown's Trading Post and famous Oak Tree may have been sites used for Jacob Brown - Cherokee Indian meetings and talks, but that the actual lease-treaty-meet with the Cherokee signing was at the home of John McDowell near Morganton, North Carolina. This information was gained from depositions in a law suit filed between John McDowell and Ruth Brown (Jacob Brown's widow) after Brown's death. Other records indicate that McDowell furnished food for over three hundred Indians during this Treaty. (See *Tennessee Historical Quarterly* September, 1962, "Jacob Brown of Nolichucky" by Paul Fink.)

The Wataugans realized that there was immediate need for a law and order control organization in their settlement. Apparently, soon after securing their ten year lease from the Indians, they organized the *Watauga Association*, thought to be the first political body organized in America free and independent of any other government rule.

The Wataugans had agreed there would be no further encroachment on Indian land when they signed the lease agreements. There was also a sort of understanding that the Cherokee would continue hunting in that territory. The quiet years of the early 1770s, plus the magic lure of the Overmountain country, brought hordes of emigrants across the mountains. Little attention was paid to boundary lines, and the woods were soon filled with white hunters. The Cherokee became greatly disenchanted with the lease arrangements, especially those who had opposed the plan from the beginning. They began complaining loudly to both Cameron and Stuart. Stuart wrote to Josiah Martin, Governor of North Carolina, about the matter; and Governor Martin sent a message across the mountains to the Wataugans, ordering them to move back inside the treaty lines or else. The Wataugans, gradually growing stronger, knew that Martin would not raise an army to cross the mountains, so they simply ignored the orders.

Another very serious incident did upset the Watauga people. Sycamore Shoals was a natural and central spot for horse racing; and a big race was planned for the spring of 1774. A large crowd had assembled for the occasion, including a sizeable number of young Indians. William Crabtree from Wolf Hills, a roughneck Indian hater, was also present. A brother or cousin of Crabtree is said to have been killed near Cumberland Gap when accompanying the Daniel Boone party of five families enroute to Kentucky to start a settlement; and Crabtree was out to kill any Indian just to get even. His chance came in the person of Cherokee Billy, a cousin of Chief Ostenaco. This murder put a damper on the festival and sent the Indians hurrying home.

Afraid that the Indians might retaliate, the Wataugans again called on James Robertson to serve as peacemaker. Robertson took with him William Falling, an Indian trader, as companion and interpreter; and the two men made the long trip to Chota without incident. On arrival, they requested and received permission to speak to the Council. Through his interpreter, Robertson expressed the horror of his people that such a needless killing had occurred. Expressing his regrets and apologies to the Cherokee, he promised that the culprit would be caught and punished.

Robertson's diplomatic appeal to the Chiefs had postponed, for the time being, a bloody frontier war. The ruling Chiefs of the Council were impressed and pleased with his apology and request for continued friendship; but the young Chiefs and relatives of Cherokee Billy were not so forgiving. An attempt was made on the lives of the two Wataugans, so Robertson and Falling were spirited away to safety. Fortunately they were in the City of Refuge.

Legend hints that it was during this trip that Robertson visited Nancy Ward. There is a faint suggestion that he hid in her house until it was safe to leave. James Robertson has described Nancy Ward as "queenly and commanding," noting that her lodge was furnished in "barbaric splendor as befitted her rank in the nation."

In the fall of 1774, Richard Henderson and Nathaniel Hart paid a visit to the Cherokee nation. They were accompanied by Thomas Price, an interpreter. Henderson, who wanted to buy or lease a large tract of land lying in Kentucky and middle Tennessee, made some persuasive talks to the Council. The Chiefs were interested inasmuch as their supply of goods was always limited and they were greedy for more. The Little Carpenter was delegated as their representative to go with Henderson to Cross Creek (Fayetteville, North Carolina) and examine the proposed trade goods. Two other Indians, a male and a female, and Price went along. The Little Carpenter and his party passed through the Moravian settlement (Winston-Salem, North Carolina) on their way to Cross Creek. From Fries Moravian Records comes this notation:

> November 23, 1774. The Indian men and woman arrived today, accompanied by several white men. They were going to Col. Henderson, who they say has bought land form the Cherokees, some 300 miles square. The Indian Chief, or king as they call him, is on his way to receive payment for the Cherokee nation; this nation is not at war, but is quiet and peaceful. . . The Indians wondered much at the organ, thinking it must be alive if it could make a sound like that; the organ had to be opened for them, for they had heard children inside who sang. . . They say they are to receive 4000 pounds in goods. . . it can hardly be believed.

Attakullakulla and Henderson left Cross Creek early in January, 1775, for the long, tough trip to Sycamore Shoals. The Little Carpenter and his party accompanied the train of six wagons loaded with supplies. Another quote from Fries Moravian Records says:

> In January, 1775, Attakullakulla was in their towns in company with Col. Richard Henderson on the way to Watauga Settlement, there to consummate, at Sycamore Shoals, a treaty with the Cherokees for the purchase of a vast domain on the Cumberland River in the Tennessee Country and in the Kentucky region. The matter of establishing an Over Hill mission was broached by the Brethren. We told the Colonel that we would like to talk with him and with the Indians, and suggested going to the Gemein Saal, to which he assented. In the Saal the organ was played which he and the Indians liked very much. We then told Colonel Henderson that we would like to have the question put to the Indians whether they wished one of our Brethren to come among them to tell them of their Creator and Savior? . . . The question was put to the Indian Chief, Little Carpenter, through the interpreter, Mr. Thomas Price, and the answer was that if any one would come and teach a school for children they would be glad.

It seems from the outset that the establishment of the Moravian Settlement at Wachovia had been for the purpose of Christianizing the nearby Cherokee Indians. This was first mentioned in 1758 but the French-Indian war intervened. This was the same settlement warned by Attakullakulla in 1760 of an impending Indian attack.

Henderson and Attakullakulla had set the first of March to hold the treaty; and Indians began arriving at Sycamore Shoals as early as January. The Carpenter had likely sent a message advising the Nation of their whereabouts with the wagons and approximate time of arrival. Colonel Richard Henderson had arranged with the Wataugans to supply the Indians with beef and corn.

It was March 14th before actual negotiations started. As was their custom the Chiefs would hold their own council meets to discuss each phase of the treaty. It was during one of these council sessions that a young Chief named Dragging Canoe, son of the Little Carpenter, exploded into prominence.

DRAGGING CANOE
1732 - 1792

He has been called —

The Savage Napoleon;
A man of consequence in his Country;
A Blood Thirsty Savage;
A dedicated Cherokee Patriot.

His enemies called him "Dragon."

Dragging Canoe's common saying —

"We Are Not Yet Conquered."

Governor William Blount said, "Dragging Canoe stood second to none in his Nation."

While a young boy, this future Chief wanted to accompany his father, Attakullakulla, and a Cherokee War Party going to battle the Shawnee. Attakullakulla flatly refused the young boy permission to go; but he slipped away from home ahead of the War Party and hid in a dugout canoe he knew the warriors must use. When the warriors arrived at the portage and discovered the determined lad, there was much teasing. Attakullakulla told his son that if he could carry the canoe across the portage he could go along; so the young boy grabbed one end of the canoe and started dragging it through the sand. The excited warriors shouted encouragement, saying "Tsi.yu Gansi.ni Tsi.yu Gansi.ni," which translated means "he is dragging the canoe;" and Dragging Canoe was his name from then on.

DRAGGING CANOE RAISES HIS TOMAHAWK

Flickering flames reflected the intense interest and expectation on the faces of the old Cherokee Chiefs around the Council Circle fire. Their talk was about the proposed land sale to Richard Henderson and his Transylvania Company. The place was Sycamore Shoals on the banks of the Watauga River (Elizabethton, Tennessee). The time was March 1775. The vast tracts of land under consideration amounted to about twenty million acres. Henderson was dickering with the Indians for two large tracts of land located in Kentucky and Tennessee.

Wagons and cabins piled full of goods, guns, ammunition, clothing, blankets, mirrors, iron tomahawks, knives, trinkets, and presents appealed to the Indians' eyes. This was a great storehouse of goodies ready for taking. Too inexperienced to realize how little any one individual would receive, they merely saw the collective display.

Important Chiefs seated around the Council Circle included Attakullakulla, the honored Peace Chief of the nation; Oconostota, the Great War Lord; Savanukah, the Raven; Oconostota's nephew and hopeful successor as War Lord, Oskuah, called Old Abram of Chilhowie; Kaiyah-tahee, known as The Tassel; Scolacutta, The Hanging Maw; and Nooneteyah, called Bloody Fellow. Among the younger Chiefs sitting within the Council Circle, but up to now saying little, were Willenawah, the Great Eagle (famous for the capture of Fort Loudoun), Tanasi Warrior, Tuckasee the Terrapin, and Tsi.yu Gansi.ni, called Dragging Canoe, son of Attakullakulla. In the background were about twelve hundred Cherokee warriors, women, and children.

Attakullakulla was making his talk:

> I am an old man who has presided as chief in councils, and as president of the
> nation for more than half a century; I formerly served as agent to the King of

England on business of first importance to our nation; I crossed the big water, arrived at our destination, and was received with great distinction; had the honor of dining with His Majesty and the nobility; had the utmost respect paid to me by the great men of the white people, and accomplished my mission with success; that from long standing in the highest dignities of our nation, I claim the confidence and good faith of all and everyone in defending and supporting the rightful claims of my people to the Bloody Grounds (Kentucky), now in treaty to be sold to the white people.

Attakullakulla finished his talk. The other older Chiefs with whom he had counciled many times during past years seemed to be in agreement with his words. Henderson's plan to purchase this vast territory from the Indians seemed headed for success. He was ready to set the day and hour for deed signing.

Suddenly, the peace of the Cherokee Council was shattered. Dragging Canoe rose to his feet, mad and disappointed. He saw through the deception being perpetrated on his people; and he was angry with his father and other Chiefs who were so willing to barter their lands away for a few cheap goods and trinkets. This six-foot-tall Chief was the head man of Amo-yeli-egwa, Great Island Town. His face, pock scarred from smallpox in his youth, scowled at those present. A hush of sudden stillness swept through the crowd. This forty-three-year-old Chief was not afraid to stand up and speak his mind in the presence of his peers. These old men were about to sign away the Hunting Grounds of the Cherokee, their only source of meat.

Scenes from an outdoor production of *The Overmountain Men* by Pat Alderman: left, Dragging Canoe delivering historic speech during Transylvania Treaty 1775; and right, Richard Henderson addressing the Council of Chiefs.

Dragging Canoe began his talk by describing the strength of the Cherokee and the flourishing state of the Nation. He spoke of the white man's encroachment on Indian lands everywhere. His voice grew louder and stronger as the crowd moved in closer to hear his words. "Whole Indian Nations have melted away like snowballs in the sun before the white man's advance. They leave scarcely a name of our people except those wrongly recorded by their destroyers. Where are the Delawares?" he shouted! "They have been reduced to a mere shadow of their former greatness. We had hoped that the white men would not be willing to travel beyond the mountains. Now that hope is gone. They have passed the mountains, and have settled upon Cherokee land. They wish to have that usurpation sanctioned by treaty. When that is gained, the same encroaching spirit will lead them upon other land of the Cherokees. New cessions will be asked. Finally the whole country, which the Cherokees and their fathers have so long occupied, will be demanded, and the remnant of Ani-Yunwiya, *The Real People*, once so great and formidable, will be compelled to seek refuge in some distant wilderness. There they will be permitted to stay only a short while, until they again behold the advancing banners of the same greedy host. Not being able to point out any further retreat for the miserable Cherokees, the extinction of whole race will be proclaimed. Should we not therefore run all risks, and incur all consequences, rather than submit to further loss of our country? Such treaties may be alright for men who are too old to hunt or fight. As for me, I have my young warriors about me. We will have our lands. A-WANINSKI, I have spoken."

Dragging Canoe finished, wrapped his blanket around his body, and walked away from the Council Grounds. The old Chiefs, greatly stirred by Dragging Canoe's impassioned plea, closed the Council session without more talk.

Henderson and his partners were greatly upset with this turn of events. They realized that quick action must be taken to overcome the powerful influence of Dragging Canoe's talk. Their big gamble to obtain the signatures of the Chiefs on deeds was threatened with failure. Henderson made arrangements for another big feast, with servings of rum for the Indians, before he and his partners presented more persuasive talks and displayed the trade goods and trinkets in an elaborate showing.

Attakullakulla, despite his son's pleading talk and persuasive argument, advised his brother Chiefs to accept Henderson's offer. Oconostota, now getting old, depended on the Raven's opinion and advice on many matters. The Raven, with strong hopes of attaining Oconostota's position as War Chief, told the Old Chief to sign. The Raven was jealous of Dragging Canoe's growing power and popularity among the young warriors.

Henderson won his gamble and March 17th was set for the deed signing. The head Chiefs of the Cherokee and other officials held the center of the stage as the hour arrived. The interpreter, Joseph Vann, read the treaty first in English and then in Cherokee. He tried to explain its full meaning to the Indians, not wanting to be blamed later for any action they might take. Vann warned the Indians that they were signing away a vast portion of their hunting grounds. Despite this warning, and ignoring Dragging Canoe's opposition, the Chiefs made their marks and their signatures were witnessed.

The Transylvania Agreement was denounced by the Royal Governors, Dunsmore of Virginia and Martin of North Carolina. The Earl of Dunsmore issued a proclamation against the land sale calling it "the unwarrantable and illegal designs of said Henderson and his abettors." The Cherokee were threatened with the King's displeasure if the transaction was not repudiated. All proclamations and threats against the Indians and frontier settlements by the British Officials concerning the Transylvania Agreement were soon thwarted by the rising tide of the American Revolutionary War.

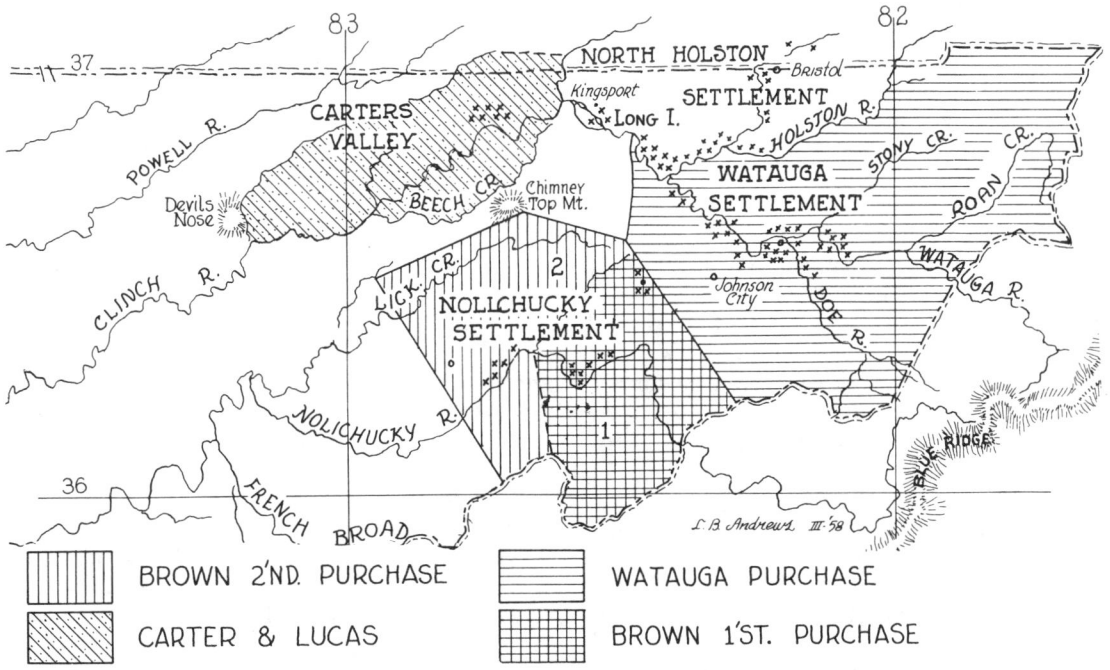

March 19th, two days after the *Great Deed* and *Path Deeds* were signed, the Watauga Association obtained grants for lands along the Watauga, Holston, and New Rivers. This has been called *The Watauga Purchase*. Charles Robertson was appointed to serve as trustee. About a week later, March 25th, Jacob Brown arranged to obtain a signed deed title to lands lying along both sides of the Nolichucky River where a sizeable settlement was already established.

Henderson wasn't through. Desiring full control of the paths to his purchase, he made another talk. "I have more goods, guns, and ammunition that you have not seen. There is land between where we stand and Kaintuckee. I do not like to walk over the land of my brothers; I want to buy from you the Road to Kaintuckee."

The angry Dragging Canoe could stand it no longer. He sprang to his feet and stomped the ground, pointing toward the lands already deeded to Henderson and Company as he spoke. "We have given you this, why do you ask for more? You have bought a fair land. When you have this you have all. There is no more game left between the Watauga and the Cumberland. There is a cloud hanging over it. You will find its settlement dark and bloody."

The infuriated Chief then stalked out of the meeting and immediately headed back to the Overhills and his home town. Several other young Chiefs, headmen, and warriors followed. They were quick to sense the new leadership ability and stability of this young Chief who dared speak out and fight for their rights. From that day until his death in 1792, Dragging Canoe never attended another Cherokee-American Treaty. He refused to sign any deeds of barter or trade with white frontier officials. Consistent with his announced intention of making the settlements of the sold lands "dark and bloody," he followed the warpaths to white communities for seventeen years. He became the savage scourge of the ever growing log cabin settlements as he planned, led, and directed his warriors through a bloody period of warfare in his determination to hold on to Cherokee culture and land.

WAR DRUMS

During the ten years following the Transylvania land transaction at Sycamore Shoals in March 1775, history has recorded: patriots fighting for the birth of a new nation, the United States; the rise of the new militant Cherokee War Chief, Dragging Canoe; and the emergence of an outstanding Indian woman, the Cherokee Chieftainess Nancy Ward. All fought for the survival of their country in their own individual ways.

Undoubtedly, British officials planned to use the Cherokee Indians to help them fight the American Rebels. The American Revolution exploded into open warfare during 1775 and quickly spread from New Hampshire to Georgia. Royal Governors fled from the colonies to the safety of British warships; and as the English government collapsed, American Patriots took over. Even Captain John Stuart, British Indian Superintendent in the South, had to flee from Charleston to the safety of St. Augustine, Florida.

The confused Cherokee became dramatically aware of political changes when their supplies were suddenly cut off at Charleston during the summer of 1775. It was difficult for them to understand why their white brothers, who came from the same country and spoke the same language, were fighting each other. Nonetheless, they were soon caught up in the whirlwinds of passions generated by this war for freedom. English agents spoke words of hope to them about getting their hunting grounds back; and the Indians, especially young warriors, were eager listeners.

The British were not about to give up their American holdings without a struggle. Plans and forces were being mobilized to subdue the rebellious subjects; and some of these plans certainly included Cherokee participation. It is only natural to assume that Captain John Stuart managed to get word to his Overhill friends at Chota as to his whereabouts. Early January, 1776, sixty-two Chiefs and warriors showed up in St. Augustine, Florida, for a visit and talks. Accompanied by Henry Stuart, younger brother of John, they left with sixty pack horses loaded with ammunition and other requested supplies. Soon after their departure, Stuart wrote Lord Dartmouth assuring him of the Cherokee's continued loyalty to the King.

Southern Patriots were not exactly idle. They were aware of the Cherokee visit to Stuart and the sixty-pack-horse loads of ammunition they took back to the Nation. When the new Continental Congress was informed of this development, they immediately appointed a Commission to visit the Cherokee towns, bearing presents and an invitation to attend a Treaty-meet at Fort Charlotte, located near Salisbury, North Carolina. The Americans were hoping to persuade the Cherokee to remain neutral during the conflict; but the Overhill Indians declined to attend the meet.

British Governors, Martin of North Carolina and Campbell of South Carolina, persuaded the British Army officials that the South was more vulnerable for conquest than the North because of the large population of Tories (British sympathizers). General Clinton decided to set up a Beach-Head near the mouth of Cape Fear River (Wilmington, North Carolina), where he landed nearly three thousand troops and established his headquarters camp. Admiral

Parker sailed from England with a fleet of forty warships to assist Clinton. Captain John Stuart was summoned by ship to Clinton's Wilmington headquarters, where it is almost certain that plans were made to synchronize Stuart's (Indians) part in the projected campaigns. Colonel Donald McDonald, commander of a sizeable Scottish force located at Cross Creek (Fayetteville, North Carolina), was instructed to march his men to Wilmington to join Clinton.

All of this looked like bad medicine for the American Patriots; however, the best of plans and schemes can go amiss and fail. Colonels James Moore, Alexander Lillington, and Richard Caswell, with their militiamen, met the two thousand Scotsmen at Moore's Creek Bridge. There they completely routed and defeated the kilted force. When Clinton received news of this disaster, he loaded his men aboard ships and moved back out to sea. Upon arrival in American waters, Admiral Parker joined Clinton; and they decided to make the next move against Charleston, South Carolina. Arriving at their destination, Clinton landed three thousand of his troops on Long Island in readiness to occupy Charleston when Parker had bombarded the town into submission.

The British had not anticipated Colonel Moultrie's valiant defense of the small fort guarding Charleston's harbor. Moultrie had only 435 men to defend the Palmetto Log Fort, with thirty cannons and twenty-eight rounds of ammunition for the cannons. One regiment of sharpshooters, under Colonel Isaac Huger, was placed in rifle pits on James Island as a second line of defense. This small American force was to prove disastrous to Parker's Navy and Clinton's plans to invade the South.

The British warships began bombarding the small Fort at daybreak June 28, 1776. Moultrie had instructed his gunners to wait until the smoke had cleared from the warships' gunfire before aiming and firing their own guns. Every shot must count. The battle continued all day. Parker's flagship was hit on the quarterdeck by an American shot, wounding Admiral Parker, Governor Campbell, and several others. One ship, hit in the powder storeroom, blew up; others were grounded. More than two hundred British Tars were killed and wounded. At dusk, Parker's badly battered fleet moved out, picked up the three thousand troops on Long Island, and left the South Carolina coast.

The American victory at Moore's Creek Bridge and the unsuccessful attempt to take Charleston upset British time tables. These two events postponed further action in the South for almost two years. Cherokee entrance into this early southern phase of the Revolution seems to have been based on expected victories of the coastal invasions. Both failed.

Some movements, once started, are hard to stop. The war fever generated among the young warriors of the Cherokee Nation was just such a movement. Thus, after the failure of the British to successfully invade the Carolina coasts, English agents in the Nation evidently wanted to cool down the war spirit they had inspired. This proved more than difficult. Dragging Canoe had spent much time visiting the Lower, Valley, and Middle Towns gaining followers for his cause. He was not about to give up his dreams of regaining their land.

The following recorded items can be interpreted to prove that a conspiracy to use the Indians had actually existed —

> John Stuart had earlier reported to General Clinton, "I do not despair of getting them (Cherokee) to act for His Majesty's service when it becomes necessary."
>
> Stedman (a later historian who was with Clinton's force in 1776) wrote, "British agents were again employed in engaging the Indians to make a diversion and enter the Southern Colonies on their backside and defenseless parts."
>
> General Gage had earlier written John Stuart, "We need not be tender of calling upon the savages to take up the hatchet against His Majesty's rebellious Subjects in America."

Later evidence seems to point to the fact that English agents were now trying to slow Dragging Canoe's war plans against the frontier settlers, until plans could be made to coordinate a British-Indian attack that had some chance of succeeding. John Stuart sent a message to the Cherokee informing them that his brother, Henry Stuart, had been appointed as Special Deputy to work with the Cherokee and that he was arranging to bring supplies from their depot at Pensacola, Florida. This news seemed to satisfy the older ruling Chiefs of the Council. They did not want war, so they were willing to wait and listen to Stuart's advice and let matters take their natural course.

This attitude didn't please Dragging Canoe, who was still mad about the land sale at Sycamore Shoals and the continued encroachment of whites on Cherokee lands. When Stuart arrived at Pensacola, he found the impatient Canoe and some eighty warriors waiting. Dragging Canoe began complaining about white encroachments and their disregard for boundary lines set by the King. He said, "The white men have almost surrounded us, leaving only a little spot of ground to stand upon, and it seems to be their intention to destroy us as a Nation." Stuart reminded Dragging Canoe that "the Indians themselves were to blame for selling their lands to Henderson without the consent or knowledge of the King's agent." Dragging Canoe replied, "I had nothing to do with making that bargain; it was made by some old men, who are too old to hunt or fight. As for me, I have a great many of my young warriors around me, and they mean to have their lands."

Superintendent John Stuart had written his brother these words: "Henry, you will understand that an indiscriminate attack on the Province is not meant, but to act in the execution of any concerted plan, and to assist His Majesty's troops and friends in distressing the Rebels and bringing them to a sense of their duty." Thus it seems the English still planned to use the Cherokee but did not want a haphazard attack on the frontiers until they (the English) were ready.

Henry Stuart was able to persuade Dragging Canoe to delay further action until he (Stuart) had time to make efforts to move the Wataugans off by peaceful means. Stuart wrote a letter to the Wataugans which demanded that they move and gave them forty days to make their arrangements. He also wrote a letter to the Tories which is said to have caused problems. Stuart, in his English reports, states that his letter to the Loyalists fell into Rebel hands and was altered to read, "an English Army was on its way from Pensacola with fifteen hundred Creeks, Choctaws and Chickasaws, to be joined by the entire force of the Cherokee Nation; which formidable army would fall on the Watauga settlements and destroy them unless they were promptly removed."

Needless to say, both fact and rumor soon spread through the Overmountain settlements. The threat of an invasion started a surge of fort building. Two companies of Overmountain militia went thought the settlements visiting some seventy Tory families, forcing them either to sign the pledge of allegiance to the American cause, leave, or be executed. Some signed; others moved. A few who resisted were shot.

Virginia officials eventually responded to the Wataugans' request for powder, lead, and military assistance. The Virginians also wrote a tart letter to the Cherokee which was delivered by Isaac Thomas. It was a message threatening an invasion by an American force from Virginia. When Thomas arrived in Chota he was asked to read the Virginia letter to the Council. Thomas also added a rumor of his own, perhaps for the hopeful purpose of discouraging Dragging Canoe's war plans. Thomas said, "The Virginians had a force of several thousand men which had been assembled to aid the Carolinians against the attempted coastal invasions. Since the British attempt had failed they were now making ready to march that force toward the Cherokee towns for the purpose of destroying the Overhill Settlements."

The older Chiefs and Stuart attempted to persuade Dragging Canoe to wait until the Cherokee and British forces could plan a cooperative attack that had some chance of succeeding. Dragging Canoe replied, "It would have been better to have attacked the Wataugans at once, without writing those letters. The letters served only to put them on guard, and caused them to prepare to come against the Cherokee. By this time they will have all their people removed. *YOU TOLD US TO ASSIST THE KING.* Now when there is a white army planning to come against our towns, we want to keep them back."

It was just a few weeks after the Wataugans received Stuart's notice to move off Indian land that a new element entered the Cherokee war picture. A delegation of fourteen Northern Chiefs arrived at Chota. These Chiefs represented the Iroquois, Mohawks, Delaware, Ottawas, Nantucas, Shawnee, and Mingo. They wanted to form a Federation of all Eastern Tribes for the purpose of resisting further encroachment on Indian lands. The visitors asked to be heard by the Cherokee Council. A time was set ten days later for the *Grand Talks*. The visitors had also requested that the Headmen in every Cherokee town be notified.

On the appointed "talk" day the Council House was filled. The flag pole and war posts had been painted red and black. After opening ceremonial rituals were finished, the Mohawk Chief spoke. He told of continued tragedies brought to his people by the whites. At the close of his talk he proffered his war belt, which was promptly accepted by Dragging Canoe. The Ottawa Chief spoke next; and when he offered his belt, it too was accepted by Dragging Canoe. The talk of the Delaware was much the same as the other Chiefs. All were asking the Cherokee to join the Federation now being organized to oppose the white frontier settlements. The Delaware belt was accepted by the Raven of Chota, nephew of Oconostota.

The final talk was made by Cornstalk, the great Chief of the Shawnee. He said:

In a few years, the Shawnee, from being a great Nation have been reduced to a handful. They once possessed land almost to the seashore, but now have hardly enough ground to stand upon.

The lands where the Shawnee have but lately hunted are covered with forts and armed men. When a fort appears, you may depend upon it there will soon be towns and settlements of white men. It is plain that the white people intend to wholly destroy the Indians. It is better for the red men to die like warriors than to diminish away by inches. The cause of the red men is just, and I hope that the Great Spirit who governs everything will favor us.

Then Cornstalk, the Great Shawnee Chief, produced his beautiful purple war belt, nine feet long and six inches wide. To dramatize this closing part of his talk, he had poured vermilion (red) paint over the belt to represent the blood of war. He then held the war belt out for acceptance. The moment of decision had arrived. A quiet stillness seemed to hover over the Council Room as Dragging Canoe rose to accept the challenge. As the Canoe stood holding the great belt, an air of suspense, lasting minutes, seemed to hold the assembled Indians spellbound. Osioota of Chilhowie stood up, advanced to Dragging Canoe's side, and took the belt as a token that he, too, accepted the challenge. He raised his tomahawk and struck the war pole, then, holding the belt above his head, began to sing their ancient war song.

A Translation of the War Song
Caw Waw Noo Dee

Where'er the earth's enlighten'd by the sun, Moon shines by night, grass grows, or waters run,
Be't known that we are going, like afar, In hostile fields to wage destructive war;
Like men we go, to meet our Country's foes, Who woman-like, shall fly our dreaded blows;
But when we go, who knows which shall return, When growing dangers rise with each new morn?
Farewell, ye little ones, yet tender wives, For you alone we would conserve our lives!
But cease to mourn, 'tis unavailing pain, If not fore-doom'd, we soon shall meet again.
But, O ye friends! in case your comrades fall, Think that on you our deaths for vengeance call;
With uprais'd tomahawks pursue our blood, and stain, with hostile streams, the conscious wood,
That pointing enemies may never tell the boasted place where we, their victims, fell.

[Some lines of the War Song as translated by one of the interpreters for Timberlake at Chota, 1762]

As Osioota ended his song, the subdued rhythmic thump of war drums began to vibrate through the stillness. A hypnotic spell seemed to sweep across the packed Council House. Osioota began moving his feet and swaying his body to the savage rhythmic beat of the drums. He circled the room holding the belt above his head. One by one the warriors and Chiefs fell in behind Osioota, picking up the rhythmic dance steps until the Council building was filled with frenzied dancers. As the number of dancers increased, so had the intensity of the drum beats. The Indians were dancing with wild abandon; their *war whoops* rang through the air with dire foreboding.

During the Council meet and dance, the older Chiefs sat in dejected silence. They had refused to accept the proffered war belts brought by the visitors, just as they had opposed Dragging Canoe's projected war. Records do not say so, but most likely Nancy Ward was present with the older Chiefs, listening and watching. Nancy and the old ones could remember an earlier War Council vote to fight the English whites, and the resulting calamities their decision had brought to the nation.

The next day Dragging Canoe, dressed in war paint, approached Henry Stuart. Angry and defiant with the English agent, he asked why the white traders had left Indian towns. Stuart replied that they were afraid for their lives and had hid in the woods. The Canoe then asked Stuart why he himself was preparing to leave Chota, and he accused Stuart for the trouble brought to the Cherokee by the threat of the Virginians. He also told Stuart that his letters to the Wataugans had started their trouble. Stuart finally forced Dragging Canoe to admit that he alone had instigated the present war movement through the Nation. Dragging Canoe then openly boasted of his leadership in the present war plans and proclaimed publicly, "Now was the time to drive the whites off their land."

Stuart then told the Indians, "I will not sanction a war that is likely to bring destruction to the Cherokee Nation. If you must go to war do not cross boundary lines nor kill women and children. Take care not to harm those who are loyal to the King (Tories)."

NANCY WARD SENDS WARNING

The four white traders, led by Isaac Thomas, slipped out of Chota sometime during the day or night of July 8, 1776, carrying Nancy Ward's message of warning to the Overmountain settlements. They reached Fort Lee (Limestone, Tennessee) July 11, ten days before Old Abram's attack on Fort Watauga and nine days before Dragging Canoe's battle at Island Flats (Kingsport, Tennessee). The warning of an imminent Indian attack on the Holston, Watauga, and Nolichucky people was not a surprise. Such a move had been anticipated for some time, and special efforts had been made to ready the forts and stockades for the expected onslaught. The timely warning did give women and children ample time to reach the nearest fort for protection.

Any speculation about Nancy Ward's reasons for sending the warning message to the whites is pure conjecture. However, recorded words, actions and written documents regarding her later years, reveal some clues to her purposes and thinking. One of Nancy's most common sayings was, "The white men are our brothers. The same house shelters us, and the same sky covers us all." Her cry was *ALL FOR PEACE*.

Nancy Ward attained her high rank as a *Cherokee Woman Chieftainess* or *Honored Woman* as a result of her action during the Cherokee-Creek Battle at Taliwa in 1755. Nonetheless, years of experience in the Nation's Council of Chiefs and constant contact with the whites had given her practical opportunities to learn the difference between intertribal warfare involving forces of her own race and wars waged between white armies and Indian warrior forces. Nancy's warning message could have been intended as a means of saving Cherokee lives as well as whites. Who knows?

Later life studies sort of indicate that Nancy believed her people needed to know more of the white man's ways and style of living in order to deal with them as equals. She was already demonstrating in her own home life how Indian families could raise cattle, clothing, and food supplies rather than depend on diminishing hunting grounds.

Nancy Ward was all Indian and, by Cherokee standards, was neither saint nor sinner. The welfare of her people seems to have been the dominating purpose in her official actions and life. She was not a figment of historical imagination but an actual human being who possessed a strong personality and character capable of enduring the problems of her country along with her people. She was not a traitor, but a fighter - in her own way - for human rights.

DRAGGING CANOE DEFEATED

The number of Overhill warriors taking the war trail for the Holston, Nolichucky, and Watauga settlements is said to have been about seven hundred. Their overall plan was to divide into three separate forces, with Dragging Canoe leading the largest force against the settlements near Long Island and the lower parts of Virginia. Chief Old Abram was to sweep through the Nolichucky and Watauga valleys; while Chief The Raven, with the smallest force, was to destroy the westernmost settlements of Carter's Valley.

The Raven and his band had split off from the main force at the Big Bend of the Nolichucky. Dragging Canoe and Old Abram continued on to unfinished Fort Lee, located on Limestone Creek not far from its junction with the Nolichucky. They found no whites since they had fled to the nearest forts. After destroying the unfinished stockade, Dragging Canoe and his warriors separated from Old Abram and moved on toward Long Island. There they met the Pioneer Force from Eaton Station in the fierce *Battle of Island Flats* (Kingsport, Tennessee) July 20, 1776.

When the Cherokee force made their attack against the five combined companies of militiamen, the captains quickly led their companies into pre-planned battle positions. This maneuvering caused Dragging Canoe to make a big mistake. Thinking the whites were retreating, The Canoe sounded his battle cry, "The Unacas are running; come on and scalp them." Theodore Roosevelt's *Winning of the West* states, "The Indian front was formed very curiously, their center being cone shaped while their wings curved outward." Captain James Shelby was the first to recognize this as a flanking movement and, realizing the danger to his comrades, pulled his company back to a higher elevation from which he could make a counterattack. This move by Shelby upset the Indian plan of battle, preventing a disastrous situation for the Holston militiamen and making the difference in the outcome of the *Battle of Island Flats*.

Dragging Canoe's warriors were met with a devastating blast of gunfire from the frontier hunter sharpshooters. Many braves, including Chief Dragging Canoe himself, fell victim to their marksmanship. The battle was of short duration and much of it at close quarters, including some hand-to-hand struggles. The confused warriors soon realized their desperate situation; and when they saw their Chief fall, they picked up their wounded and fled the battlefield.

It was a depressed band of Cherokee warriors that arrived back at their temporary camp. Dragging Canoe, wounded in the thigh, was greatly humiliated at this inglorious defeat by the white Virginians. His great plan was ending in dismal failure, with thirteen of his warriors killed, several more wounded, including himself, and not one white scalp to show for the battle.

THE RAVEN OF CHOTA

The smaller division of warriors, led by Chief The Raven, followed the Great War Trail from the Big Bend of the Nolichucky on across the Holston River and into the Carter's Valley settlements (now Hawkins County, Tennessee). Here they found most of the settlers had either moved into the safety of the forts or left for Virginia. Raven split his force into several small bands with instructions to search, loot, and destroy.

One of the raiding bands came upon Jonathan Mulkey, a Baptist preacher working in the field with an unnamed companion. Mulkey somehow managed to escape and reached the Holston River where he swam to safety. His companion, not so lucky, was caught, knocked down, scalped, and left for dead. Mulkey finally made his way through the woods to Eaton's Fort. Imagine his surprise, on arriving at the stockade, to find his companion had reached the fort ahead of him, minus his scalp.

Another of The Raven's small bands had continued on into Virginia as far as Wolf's Hills (Abingdon). They came upon the Reverend Charles Cummings and William Creswell, enroute to church on a wagon pulled by a team of horses. Creswell was killed; but Cummings managed to beat off the assailants and drive the wagon (carrying Creswell's unscalped body) to safety. It is said that the Reverend Cummings made a habit of taking his rifle, powder, and shot with him to all church services; and during the preaching hour his loaded gun always stood near the altar.

OLD ABRAM AND FORT WATAUGA

Chief Old Abram set up his camp on the north bank of the Nolichucky River, not far from the home site of Jacob Brown. The Chief then led his warriors along the foothills toward the Watauga Settlement. Most of the settlers in that area had already reached the security of the fort. According to William Tatham, a member of the fort command, about seventy-five male defenders were inside the Watauga Stockade. Officers in command were Colonel John Carter, Captain James Robertson and Lieutenant John Sevier.

Abram made his first attack against the fort in the early morning hours of July 21. It is said that some of the women, who had gone outside the garrison to milk the cows, were first to discover the Indians. Their screams, as they ran for the fort gates, alerted the men who quickly manned the walls.

During the confusion of this first Indian charge, the gates were closed before one woman could get inside. This young lady was Catherine Sherrill, a tall athletic girl who, with her family, had arrived at the fort early. It is said that she could outride, outshoot, and outrun almost any man in the settlement. As Catherine ran for the gate she saw that some warriors had managed to get between her and the gate entrance, so she turned toward the nearest side wall. She was determined, as she later said, "to scale the fort wall in spite of the bullets and arrows which came like hail. It was leap or die as I would not live a captive." As she made ready to leap for the top, a hand reached down to aid and a voice shouted "Jump for me, Kate!" The man who pulled Catherine Sherrill to safety and four years later married the famous "Bonnie Kate" was John Sevier.

After the first unsuccessful attack, Chief Abram pulled his warriors back out of gun range and set up siege positions around the fort. Days later, during the seeming absence of Indians, James Cooper and Samuel Moore slipped out of the fort on a harmless mission; but they were caught near the mouth of Gap Creek. Cooper, attempting to escape across the river, was shot and scalped.

Moore was taken captive and conducted to Abram's Nolichucky camp. Except for occasional sniper fire, no more attacks were attempted; however, a group of some twenty-five braves did attempt to set the fort walls on fire. They might have succeeded had not Ann Robertson and the other women been alert. They used boiling water from their washpots to pour down on the Indians who, with screams of pain, soon withdrew.

Old Abram, discouraged by the strong defense put up by fort riflemen and the news of Dragging Canoe's defeat at Island Flats, decided to call off the siege. News of a Virginia relief force marching to aid the Watauga people hastened his departure.

POWER OF LIFE AND DEATH

After Old Abram had set up his temporary camp on the Nolichucky, he sent several small bands of warriors out to search for food, as well as to loot and capture any whites. One band of braves came upon Mrs. William Bean, who had been late leaving her home for the Watauga Fort. She was captured and taken prisoner to the Nolichucky camp.

A white trader who had accompanied the Indians on this campaign as interpreter was told to question their white captives. The interpreter told Mrs. Bean that she was to be killed; and, as he spoke, a warrior cocked his gun and held it in a threatening manner. The Chief, through the trader, asked about the number of forts in the area. Could the people inside be starved into submission? Did they have food and water? How many white soldiers were in the Forts? Not easily intimidated, Mrs. Bean told the Chief that the settlers had enough men, guns, powder, and lead to stop any attack, and sufficient food and water to last a long time.

When Chief Old Abram lifted the siege and returned to the Overhill Towns, he took Mrs. Bean and Samuel Moore along as prisoners of war. The two white captives and two or three scalps were about the only spoils of war he could take back to show his people. Mrs. Bean was imprisoned at Toqua, a town near Chota. Young Samuel Moore was carried off to Tuskegee, where he was tortured in barbaric, savage ways before being burned at the stake.

Mrs. William Bean, when her time came, was taken to a mound where an upright stake-pole was buried near the center. She was tied to this pole with leather thongs; then dry tree branches were laid around her feet and lighted. Nancy Ward, having learned of the planned torture and burning, suddenly appeared. Going up on the mound, she kicked the burning brands away, stomped out the remaining small flames, and cut the thongs, freeing Mrs. Bean.

Then, turning to the angered warriors, she spoke with harsh words, "It revolts my soul that Cherokee warriors would stoop so low as to torture a squaw. No woman shall be tortured or burned at the stake while I am *Honored Woman.*" (This is a historically recorded incident of Nancy Ward's exercising her official position as *Ghighau*, one who has power of life and death over condemned prisoners.)

Nancy led Mrs. Bean down from the mound, through the angry glaring warriors, and took her to her home in Chota, the Town of Sanctuary. She asked Mrs. Bean to teach her and members of her family how to process cow's milk to make butter and cheese. Nancy had evidently started her own small herd, anxious to interest her people in raising their own meat and farm crops, rather than depending on the dwindling wildlife of the forests and the traders' expensive supplies that had to be hauled in on pack horses.

When it was safe to do so, Nancy Ward sent Mrs. Bean back to her home on the Watauga River. Nancy's son Five Killer and her brother Long Fellow accompanied Mrs. Bean to protect her during the long journey.

DESTRUCTION OF MIDDLE, VALLEY, AND LOWER SETTLEMENTS

Dragging Canoe's defeat at Island Flats could have taught him a valuable lesson. Historical records indicate Indians were not conditioned emotionally and lacked needed discipline to combat white armies in open battle formations. This young War Chief evidently decided to stick to the old Indian style of warfare — surprise, attack, scalp, and disappear. Dragging Canoe also realized he could not return home a defeated leader. He had nothing to show from his battle but thirteen dead warriors and several wounded, including himself.

Unable to travel, The Canoe sent several small parties into scattered areas of Powell, Clinch, and Holston valleys with instructions to raid, loot, kill, and scalp. Those warrior bands returned with eighteen white scalps, some loot, and a few horses. By Indian standards, Dragging Canoe had turned his defeat into a sort of victory.

About the same time as the Nolichucky-Watauga-Holston-Carter valley attacks, warrior bands form the Middle, Valley, and Lower Cherokee settlements were raiding and harassing the Georgia and Carolina frontiers. While pursuing a band of marauding Indians from the Lower towns, one company of Georgia Militia, under Lieutenant Grant, was drawn into an ambush, captured, and tortured. Grant's body was later found tied to a tree, with scalp and ears cut off; and a gun barrel, supposed to have been red hot, had been thrust into his body. Twelve arrows were sticking in his chest; and above them lay a painted war club. A war-decorated tomahawk was stuck into the tree above his head. The men who discovered the body were so affected by the scene they fled in panic. [British Colonial Papers]

Cherokee raiding parties ravaged white border settlements located in the western sections of the two Carolinas and North Georgia. Records indicate that Alexander Cameron himself led some of the attacks. On one occasion, Cameron is reported to have led a force of two hundred — Tories, dissident Creeks, and Cherokee — into the settlements of western South Carolina, returning with many white scalps of men, women, and children.

This ruthless period of Indian raids on southern frontiers caused angry waves of resentment to sweep through the white colonies. The raids did more to unite frontier settlers against the British and their Indian allies than any possible fear of the King's detested red-coated troops could have done. Officials of Georgia, the Carolinas, and Virginia began active measures to carry out previously discussed plans for a simultaneous attack against the Cherokee Nation, hoping to destroy their fighting power before the British could mount another southern coastal invasion that might succeed.

Officials of all four states were made more aware of the Indian danger to their backside during the two unsuccessful coastal invasion attempts made earlier by the British; and plans to destroy the Cherokee were being talked about even before July 1776. General Griffith Rutherford, Brigadier-General of the Salisbury District of North Carolina, had been advocating such a move for some time; and he wrote North Carolina's President of the Safety Council July 5, 1776, stating, "If such a campaign can be mounted I have no doubts of the destruction of the Cherokee Nation." South Carolina officials were urging that the "Cherokee be treated as British allies and that a campaign against those savages be carried out with all possible vigor." Perhaps Dragging Canoe's talks in all sections of the Nation stimulated the frontier raids.

With a company of Georgia Militia, Colonel Samuel Jack led one of the first of the four states which hit the warpath. A thorough destruction of towns and crops along the

Chattahoochee, Tulluluh, and Tugaloo Rivers was accomplished. Few Cherokee inhabitants were killed during Colonel Jack's campaign, as they had managed to escape into the hills.

In his *Winning Of The West*, Roosevelt suggests that the angered South Carolinians came on strong. In order to raise a large volunteer army to fight the Cherokee, South Carolina officials offered £75 (seventy-five pounds English money) for every enemy scalp taken and £100 for every live prisoner delivered. South Carolina is said to have mustered a force estimated at 1,860. Colonel Andrew Williamson, with Colonel Hammond as aide, was placed in command.

Colonel Williamson had evidently reached the site of abandoned Fort Prince George in late August. Records indicate that on August 31, 1776, he sent a detachment of 350 mounted men from there, under Colonel Hammond, on a forced march to Seneca. Scouts had reported that Alexander Cameron and Dragging Canoe, with a sizable force of Indians and Tories, were encamped there.

When Colonel Hammond reached Seneca, he found the Indian houses on the east bank abandoned. The town was built up along both sides of Keowee River, so Hammond gave orders to move forward across the stream and attack the houses on the west bank. About the time the troops up front reached midstream, they were met with heavy gunfire from hidden warriors. Five white soldiers were killed, and thirteen were wounded. The surprised troops panicked and made a disorderly retreat to safety. Colonel Hammond managed to halt the fleeing men. With lashing tongue he ridiculed them and called them cowards; then, turning his horse back into the river ford, he dared the men to follow. A few accepted the challenge; then others, realizing how they had acted, began to follow. Soon all the command were charging across the river to attack the houses on the west bank where the gunners had been hidden.

Cameron and Dragging Canoe, realizing they were outnumbered and outgunned, withdrew into the hills where the women and children had been taken for safety. Dragging Canoe had evidently recovered sufficiently from his wound at Island Flats to get back into action. Cameron and Canoe had formed a close friendship and apparently had worked together in generating the four-state border war. They were sworn blood brothers.

After destroying Seneca and other neighboring settlements, Colonel Hammond headed back to rejoin the main force at Fort Prince George. Meanwhile, Colonel Williamson had sent out detachments to destroy every crop, town, and Indian found in the Lower Cherokee towns before marching toward the Valley settlements.

The South Carolina Army was making the toilsome climb up the steep and narrow trail toward Neowee Pass. As the front ranks neared the crest, a blast of heavy gunfire came from warriors hidden in protected spots alongside the trail. Seventeen whites were killed and twenty-seven were wounded during the ambush.

It was a confused, panicked force that tried to retreat downhill over a trail already crowded from behind by advancing troops; and again Colonel Hammond saved the day. Somehow he managed to halt the fleeing men and restore some semblance of order. When out of range of Indian fire, he called for volunteers to make a holding, delaying frontal attack on the hidden warriors. This force was placed under Lieutenant Hampton. Another force, to be led by Colonel Hammond himself, was selected to maneuver around the hill and make a flanking assault. This company of volunteers managed to clamber up another section of the mountainside and attack the warriors from an unprotected side. Eventually the braves were routed and the pass was cleared. It is said that it took Colonel Williamson's South Carolina force five long hard days to travel the twenty miles from Neowee Pass to the Valley Towns where he was to meet General Rutherford's North Carolina Army.

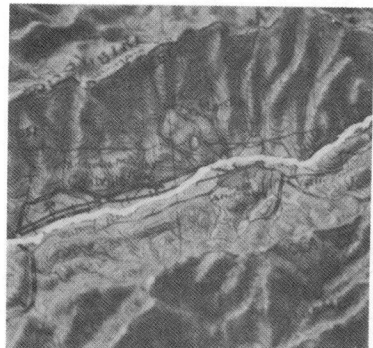 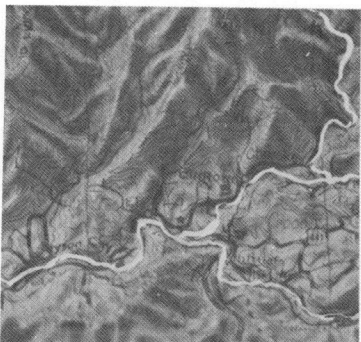 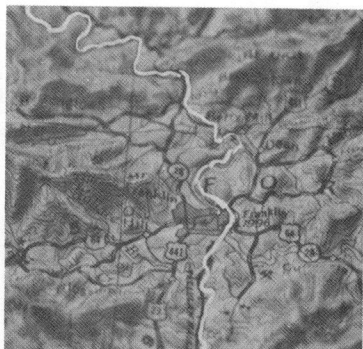

General Rutherford's command of twenty-four hundred was made up of several volunteer detachments from various locations in the Salisbury District. They rendezvoused at Davidson's Fort [Old Fort, North Carolina]. (The route of march followed by Rutherford is used here in an abbreviated form. The full account is recorded in *Myths of the Cherokee*, by James Mooney, page 205.)

The North Carolina Army crossed the Blue Ridge Mountains through Swannanoa Gap; followed Swannanoa River to its junction with the French Broad, which was crossed at Warrior Ford; traveled up Hominy Creek and across a ridge to Pigeon River; crossed this river below the junction of its east and west forks; then on to Richland Creek, and crossed said creek just above present town of Waynesville, North Carolina; crossed another ridge to head of Scott's Creek, which stream was followed over rugged mountain terrain to its junction with Tuckasegee River, which they crossed to west side; followed a main trail down west side to first Cherokee town, Stekoa (perhaps Sticoy). This town was abandoned at the approach of the army.

One detachment was sent to follow the fugitive Indians northward toward Oconaluftee River and Soco Creek. Eventually they gave up the chase, but Indian homes and small settlements found in the area were destroyed before this detachment returned to rejoin the main force. After the destruction of Sticoy, Rutherford's Army sent out detachments to lay waste all Cherokee Settlements on Tuckasegee River before crossing the dividing ridge southward of present Whittier. The Army followed Cowee Creek to the Little Tennessee River, totally destroying all homes and crops before resuming the march. After the methodical destruction of the Middle Towns, the Army ascended Cartoogechaye Creek, west of present Franklin, and crossed Nantahala Mountains at Wayah Gap. Here a body of warriors opposed their passage with a hard-fought battle, but the greatly outnumbered Indians fled after killing and wounding more than forty white troops. One Indian killed in this battle turned out to be a woman dressed, painted, and armed like a warrior. After crossing the Nantahala River, the Army continued westward across the mountains to Valley River.

Rutherford's Army and Williamson's South Carolina forces made a junction in the Valley Settlements September 26, 1776. They methodically destroyed every dwelling, cutting down or driving their horses over the food crops to destroy them. All Indian towns from the Oconaluftee to the Nottely and Hiwassee Rivers (thirty-six towns in all) were destroyed, along with the food crops. The Cherokee warrior force was just too small to attempt any strong resistance against a force numbering over four thousand men with a single purpose — destruction of the Cherokee Nation.

After completing their work of devastation and taking a short rest period, each Army returned home by pretty much the same route they had traveled to reach the Valley Settlements. Thousands of homeless Indians had been forced into the woods to starve or live as best they could. Some fled across the mountains to the uncertain safety of the Overhill Towns. Many of the Lower Town families moved westward to the upper waters of the Coosa River. The refugee Indians sought whatever sanctuary they could find. There is no known estimate of the number of Indians killed during this campaign, but records indicate that between seventy or eighty Indian scalps were turned in to the South Carolina authorities for their £75 per scalp.

CHRISTAIN'S CAMPAIGN

The Georgia-Carolinas campaign against the Lower, Valley, and Middle Cherokee Settlements was practically over and the troops headed homeward before the Virginia-Western North Carolina Army, commanded by Colonel William Christian, had proceeded very far toward the Overhill Indian Towns. The four-state undertaking had been planned as a simultaneous campaign against the Cherokee.

Lieutenant Colonel William Russell, already stationed at Long Island, decided that a fortification was needed on the Holston. The Fort, when completed, was named *Fort Patrick Henry*, after Virginia's Governor. Colonel Christian was delayed in reaching the rendezvous, as he stopped enroute to relieve wives and mothers of his troops who had been confined in forts along the Clinch and Holston Rivers. Raiding parties of Shawnee, dissident Cherokees, and Creeks were posing a constant threat to all the settlements.

The Surry County forces commanded by Colonel Joseph Williams and Major Joseph Winston arrived at Fort Patick Henry September 21, 1776. Much precaution was necessary

Fort Patrick Henry (Courtesy Max Spoden)

because of the many war parties lurking in the vicinity.

Colonel Christain's command left the Fort on the long march to Cherokee country the first week in October, 1776. The first day, they advanced six miles to *Double Springs*, near the foot of Chimney Top Mountain. There Captains James Robertson and John Sevier, with their Watauga and Nolichucky companies, joined the Christain forces. Captain John Sevier had the only mounted company in this army of 1,800 troopers; and sixteen of the mounted men were assigned to scout duty under Valentine Sevier, Jr.

A report Christain sent to Governor Henry, dated October 6, 1776, and evidently written from Double Springs Camp, reads:

I shall march in less than an hour and take with me thirty days' flour and seventy days' beef. I hope to cross [French] Broad River the 15th inst., where it is likely I shall be attacked or meet with proposals of peace. The men [traders] who have fled from the towns say the Indians will surely fight desperately; which they promised Stuart, the King's Superintendent, to do; and Cameron, his deputy, who remains amongst them as daily encouraging them to defend their country against a parcel of Rebels. I heartily wish that they may first attack me; and it is the wish of the army. Cameron, being an awful man, may invent measures to delay our march if the Indians will execute them with dexterity; but still I have no doubt of returning to the Island in five weeks from this time, six at fartherest.

Progress was slow, as the men were mainly foot soldiers; and miry ground and canebrakes made it tough going for both men and the pack horses carrying supplies. While they were camped near the mouth of Lick Creek, Ellis Harlan, a white trader, was escorted into camp. It is said Harlan had been sent by The Raven of the Cherokee Council to see if Christain would talk peace terms with the Chiefs. Harlan also told Christain that Dragging Canoe's followers were planning an ambush on the south side of the French Broad River. Colonel Christain conducted Harlan through the camp to show him the size and fire power of his force then gave him the following message to deliver to the Council of Chiefs:

How can you expect peace before you have delivered up to me Alexander Cameron, that enemy of the white men and the red? How can you ask for peace when you have assembled your men to fight me should you dislike my terms?

I shall cross the river and come to your towns. I will distinguish between those towns which have behaved well toward us, and those which have not.

Harlan's return and delivery of Christain's message set off a violent debate in the Council; and sharp divisions in opinion arose as to which course to take. Overhill Towns and homes were already crowded with refugees from the Middle and Valley Towns. The Old Chiefs wanted peace and wanted to make terms with Christain, hoping to save their beloved towns and homes. Cameron and Dragging Canoe, backed by their followers, wanted to vacate the old towns, move farther south and fight on. Thus the Cherokee Council was divided into two camps: *The Peace Party* versus *The War Party*.

The Peace Party Chiefs were blaming all their troubles and the plight of the nation on Cameron and Dragging Canoe. During the debate, Caleb Starr, a white trader and friend of the Old Chiefs, asked permission to speak. When permission was granted Starr said, "Make peace with Christain. The Cherokee cannot hope to defeat such a large and well-armed force of Americans. The Great Spirit has fore-ordained that the White Men will triumph over the Red Men... resistance will be futile."

When the talks and arguments had finally ended, the Council vote was taken. The Peace Party won. The defeated Dragging Canoe left the Council House mad but determined. He made a drastic decision: He and his followers would leave the Overhill country, move further south, set up new headquarters, organize their own Council with loyal cooperating Chiefs, and fight on. This drastic confrontation between the two opposing groups split the Cherokee Nation asunder.

Dragging Canoe and his War Party followers began moving out of their homes and towns before the Christain force reached the French Broad River. In their rush to leave, much of their household belongings and winter food supplies were left behind. The Badger and Little Owl, two other sons of the aging Attakullakulla, followed their brother Dragging Canoe. Nancy Ward's brother, Long Fellow, was another of the defectors.

The French Broad River originates in North Carolina. Mud and Cane Creeks, as well as the Davidson, Little Mills, Hominy, and Swannanoa Rivers, are tributaries. Many other streams join its flow before it meanders into Tennessee. Pioneer hunters, seeing this river for the first time, saw that it flowed toward French Territory. They called this broad stream the *French Broad*. It became a natural boundary in the settlements.

Colonel Christain's army reached the French Broad River and crossed without opposition. The march continued on to the Little Tennessee which was crossed at a ford near Toqua. Camp was made at Tomotley the night of October 18. The next day, they passed Tuskegee and the site of Fort Loudoun before halting at Great Island Town. It was here, at Dragging Canoe's abandoned home town, that Christain set up his headquarters Camp. Many of the white troops soon occupied the deserted Indian houses and appropriated the stored provisions left behind by the defecting Cherokee. Most of the Overhill towns had been evacuated and the women, children, and old folk taken into the forests for safety.

Ellis Harlan came into Christain's Camp to report the split in the Council and the hurried departure of the Dragging Canoe followers. Harlan also told of Cameron's effort to hire someone to kill both Nathaniel Gist and himself because of their efforts in trying to arrange peace talks. Colonel Christain sent a message to the Chiefs of the Peace Party, asking them to come into his camp for talks. The following letter, written by Christain to Governor Henry, tells some of the story:

> I wrote The Raven that, as he wishes to speak to me, I was now here and found that his nation would not fight; that I was willing to hear him and other Chiefs; that I did not come to war with women and children but to fight with men; that his people had better be on their guard, because if they did not comply with my terms after seeing me I should see them safe from camp and then consider them as enemies...
>
> Tomorrow I expect The Raven, Oconostota, The Carpenter and many others of the Chiefs; and I suppose in three days I can open a treaty or begin to destroy the towns and pursue the Indians toward the Creeks. I know, sir, that I could kill and take hundreds of them and starve hundreds by destroying their corn, but it would be mostly the women and children, as the men could retreat faster than I can follow, and I am convinced that Virginia State would be better pleased to hear that I showed pity to the distressed and spared the suppliants rather than that I should commit one act of barbarity in destroying a whole nation of enemies. I believe that all the old warriors and all the women of the nation this side of the Hills [The Appalachians] were adverse to the war, and that the rest were led by Cameron, sometimes by bribing them and at other times threatening them.

Chota, capital of the Cherokee Nation, Town of Sanctuary, and home of Nancy Ward and her Uncle, The Little Carpenter, was spared. Perhaps Christain remembered Attakullakulla's long friendship with the Virginians; and it could be that Nancy Ward's warning to the settlements, before the July attacks, influenced this consideration. Anyhow, the compassion shown the Overhill Cherokee was far different from the attitude displayed toward the Lower, Valley, and Middle Towns during the Carolina-Georgia campaigns. Some humane influence entered the picture from some source, because Christian's official orders included these instructions:

> Severely chastise that cruel and perfidious Nation in a manner to stop future insults and ravages. Reduce them to the necessity of suing for peace. Demand a sufficient number of Chiefs and Warriors as hostages to secure performance of the conditions you may require of them.

The Raven, acting War Chief, The Little Carpenter, Oconostota, Old Tassel, and several other friendly Headmen went to Christian's Camp for talks. The Chiefs who had participated in the frontier war against the settlers were absent.

Colonel Christian had, meanwhile, sent expeditionary forces out with orders to destroy the towns and provisions of those who were bloodguilty of the war. Two towns in particular were singled out for destruction. One was Tuskegee, where Samuel Moore was tortured to death, and the other was Toque, where Mrs. William Bean had been held prisoner and threatened with death by fire until rescued by Nancy Ward.

During the talks with the Chiefs, Christian gave them instructions which amounted to an ultimatum — "co-operate or be destroyed." Among his demands were: Dragging Canoe and Alexander Cameron should be delivered to his camp; all white prisoners in the Nation must be released; and all stolen horses must be returned to their owners. A final condition was that the State Council send an authorized delegation to Long Island in June of 1777 to meet with representatives from Virginia and North Carolina to sign an official Peace Treaty and establish boundary lines.

When questioned about Dragging Canoe and Cameron, Oconostota told Colonel Christian that Cameron had gone to Pensacola, Florida, and Dragging Canoe and his followers had split off from the Cherokee Nation and moved farther south. The Old Chief also said he and others were against the war from the beginning; that it was fought against their advice; and as War Chief he no longer had any influence over Dragging Canoe, and that the Cherokee Council could not be held responsible for The Canoe's actions.

Colonel Christian completed preliminary plans for the June Meet at Long Island. He did not ask for hostages as a guarantee of Cherokee co-operation. He did post rewards of £100 (one hundred pounds) each for the capture of Dragging Canoe and Alexander Cameron, dead or alive.

Some of the officers on Christian's staff, Colonel Joseph Williams in particular, did not agree with the leniency used in dealing with the Indians. Williams wrote a letter to the President of North Carolina's Provincial Congress, from the Indian town of Citico, stating that nothing had been done "except burning five of their towns and patched up a kind of peace.... I have this day obtained leave to return home with my battalion." [N.C. Col. Recs.]

Colonel Christian reached the Shelby home (Bristol, Tennessee) on his return to the Holston Settlements, November 12, 1776. While there, he issued a proclamation forbidding white inhabitants to enter Indian territory without permission; but such proclamations were mostly ignored by frontiersmen. Many of the troopers who had accompanied Christian had their first glimpse of the lush lands of the French Broad and Little Tennessee basins. The excitement generated and the inflow of settlers that followed is described by Ramsey in his *Annals of Tennessee*.

> Each soldier upon his return home gave a glowing account of the adaptation of the country to all purposes of agriculture. The story was repeated from one to another, till upon the Roanoke and the Yadkin the people spoke familiarly of the Holston, the Nolichucky, the French Broad, the Little River and The Tennessee. Particular places were selected, springs designated and points chosen as centres for future settlements. A flood of immigration followed to strengthen, build up and enlarge the little community already planted across the mountain.

THE LONG ISLAND TREATY

The Overhill Cherokee referred to all settlers of the Nolichucky-Watauga-Holston region as Virginians. Dragging Canoe seemed to hate these people as much as they feared him. During the big Council arguments at Chota, Dragging Canoe and Cameron had urged the Ruling Chiefs to abandon their towns on the Little Tennessee, retreat southward, and fight on. The older Chiefs could not accept the thought of seeing their beloved old home towns destroyed, so they had resisted such a move.

The angry Dragging Canoe left the Council and began putting his new plans into action. He and many of his people began moving immediately. During the winter of 1776-1777, the great exodus took place. Some families walked, carrying what they could; others packed their possessions into dugout canoes for the trip down river. Those who still owned horses made packsaddles or travois to haul their belongings to their new homes.

The sites selected for the new settlements were located on Chickamauga Creek and the Tennessee River. John McDonald, one of Stuart's deputies, was already living in that area. The new location was around the foot of Lookout Mountain (Chattanooga, Tennessee). The Indians called the mountain *Chatanuga*. The name has a Creek Indian origin: Chada (rock), Na (that), Nysa (come-to-an-end). Because of the Chickamauga Creek name and an old town site by the same name, Dragging Canoe's settlements became known as *Chickamauga*.

Colonel Christain left the Cherokee country about December 1, 1776. Cameron, meanwhile, had joined Dragging Canoe and his followers at Chickamauga. From there Cameron sent a strong message to the Overhill Chiefs, informing them that any Chief or town Headsman that dared sign treaties with the Americans would receive no English supplies. The supply list included ammunition, food, and clothing.

The preliminary peace agreement, worked out between Colonel Christain and the Overhill Chiefs, did not slow Dragging Canoe's plans to harass the Virginians. His raids in the Holston, southwest Virginia, and Clinch Valley settlements were a constant menace. This caused Governor Patrick Henry to make plans for an earlier Treaty Meet in an effort to end the turmoil. He sent Nathaniel Gist to the Cherokee country as an emissary, to arrange with the Chiefs to attend a meeting at Fort Patrick Henry in April. Gist persuaded the Overhill Chiefs to attend, but the Chickamauga Headmen wanted no part of a treaty.

The Carpenter, Oconostota, The Raven, and a delegation of eighty-five went to the Fort to talk with Governor Henry as requested. This meeting was premature, as North Carolina had not yet selected representatives to meet with the Indians. Governor Henry tried to persuade the Chiefs to become allies of the Americans. The Carpenter, speaking for the group, replied, "We cannot fight our Father King George." He reminded the Governor that Colonel Christain had promised that they could remain neutral if they signed the Peace Treaty. The months of June and July were again affirmed as the time for the *Big Meet*.

Dragging Canoe, with a price on his head, had refused to attend the April Treaty. He was busy raising havoc, raiding and scalping in the vicinity of Long Island. History records the scalping of Frederick Calvitt and massacre of the Crockett family who were living at the present site of Rogersville, Tennessee. James Robertson had several horses stolen. Dragging Canoe was keeping his promise of a "dark and bloody ground." He took many scalps home from the April raids.

The Indian scare in the Nolichucky-Watauga-Holston settlements became so bad, two companies of Militia were stationed in the Overmountain country to provide protection. One company, commanded by Benjamin Cleveland from Wilkes County, North Carolina, was quartered at Fort Watauga. Another company, thought to be under Major Jesse Walton, was stationed at Fort Williams on the Nolichucky River (near the site where John Sevier later built his home, called Mount Pleasant). Four other independent companies of rangers were organized for patrol duty. One such company, under Captain James Stuart, was assigned to patrol from Greasy Cove (Unicoi County, Tennessee) to Dungan's Mill (Watauga, Tennessee).

The Treaty Meet at Long Island on the Holston River finally started about June 28, 1777. The Meet had barely gotten under way when an unfortunate incident occurred which threatened its continuation. A large number of Cherokee had accompanied their Chiefs to the treaty grounds. Big Bullet, half-breed son of one McCormick, an interpreter, had crossed to a small river island and was at work mending his moccasins. One of the pioneers, seeing this and thinking the Indian was up to some kind of mischief, shot him. The Chiefs, informed of the incident and afraid for their own safety, left the meeting. The Commissioners offered a reward for the man who did the shooting; but it was years later before the name of the person responsible was revealed. Robert Young eventually told his brother-in-law, Valentine Sevier, about the shooting and confessed that he was the culprit.

The Virginia Commissioners chosen for the meet were Colonels Christain, Preston, and Evan Shelby. From North Carolina, Waightstill Avery, Joseph Winston, Robert Lanier, and William Sharpe attended. Special recognition and attention was given two Chiefs, Oconostota

Historic Long Island: 1) The Island; 2) Island Flats and Fort Patrick Henry (beyond the ridge); 3) Bay's Mountain; 4) Tilthammer Shoals; 5) Tilthammer Rock; 6) Indian War Path; 7) Sluice of Holston River.

and the Little Carpenter, both growing old. Two chairs were placed in prominent positions, and presents of matching coats were draped over the seats prepared for the veteran Cherokee leaders. The Commissioners reproached the Chiefs for the murders committed in the Holston and Kentucky areas during recent months. They also asked the whereabouts of Dragging Canoe and other Chiefs who were responsible for the continuation of raids on the whites. Oconostota explained that those responsible for the bloodletting had moved away from the Overhill towns and set up their own government and council at Chickamauga. "We have no influence over them and refuse to be responsible for them or their actions."

Another Treaty had taken place at Dewitts Corners, South Carolina, May 20, 1777. Georgia and South Carolina Commissioners, during this treaty with the Chiefs of the Lower and Valley Towns, had demanded large sections of Indian land on the Tugaloo, Savannah, and Saluda Rivers. South Carolina took all the Indian land in that state except a small border along the western boundary. The war, instigated by Dragging Canoe and Cameron during the summer of 1776, cost the Cherokee Nation over five million acres of land.

The aging Oconostota, who was head of the Cherokee delegation at Long Island but had never been much of a public speaker, assigned to Old Tassel the task of making the speech to the Commissioners. Following is a translated copy of his talk:

> It is surprising that when we enter into treaties with our fathers, the white people, their whole cry is more land. Indeed it has seemed a formality with them to demand what they know we dare not refuse. But on the principles of fairness of which we have received assurance during the conduct of this treaty, I must refuse your demand.
>
> What did you do? You marched into our towns with a superior force. Your numbers far exceeded us, and we fled to the stronghold of our woods, there to secure our women and children. Our towns were left to your mercy. You killed a few scattered and defenseless individuals, spread fire and desolation wherever you pleased, and returned to your own habitations.
>
> If you term this a conquest, you have overlooked the most essential point. You should have fortified the junction of Holston and Tennessee Rivers, and thereby conquered all the waters above. It is now too late for us to suffer from your mishap of generalship. Will you claim our lands by right of conquest? No! If you do, I will tell you that WE last marched over them, even up to this very place; and some of our young warriors whom we have not had opportunity to recall are still in the woods and continue to keep your people in fear.
>
> Much has been said of the want of what you term *Civilization* among the Indians. Many proposals have been made to us to adopt your laws, your religion, your manners, and your customs. We do not see the propriety of such a reformation. We should be better pleased with beholding the good effect of these doctrines in your own practices than with hearing you talk about them, or of reading your papers to us on such subjects. You say, 'Why do not the Indians till the ground and live as we do?' May we not ask with equal propriety, 'Why do not the white people hunt and live as we do?'
>
> We wish, however, to be at peace with you, and to do as we would be done by. We do not quarrel with you for the killing of an occasional buffalo or deer on our lands, but your people go much farther. They

> hunt to gain a livelihood. They kill all our game; but it is very criminal in our young men if they chance to kill a cow or a hog for their sustenance when they happen to be in your lands.
>
> The Great Spirit has placed us in different situations. He has given you many advantages, but he has not created us to be your slaves. We are a separate people! He has stocked your lands with cows, ours with buffalo; yours with hogs, ours with bears; yours with sheep, ours with deer. He has given you the advantage that your animals are tame, while ours are wild and demand not only a larger space for range, but art to hunt and kill them. They are, nevertheless, as much our property as other animals are yours, and ought not to be taken from us without our consent, or for something of equal value.

William Tatham, who translated Old Tassel's speech, says that "It was bereaved of much of its native beauty by the defects of interpretation, for the manly and dignified expression of the Indian orator loses nearly all its energy and force in translation." He describes Old Tassel as a "stout, mild, and decided man, rather comely than otherwise, who, through a long and useful life in his own country, was never known to stoop to a falsehood."

The Commissioners were so moved by the plea that they changed the terms of the Treaty to read: "Far enough down the Nolichucky River to include lands already settled." This placed the boundary line about twenty or thirty miles south of the site later selected for Jonesborough. The Long Island Treaty Meet was not voluntary on the part of the Cherokee; their plight was desperate. Their Overhill towns were crowded with refugees from the Middle and Valley Settlements who needed food and shelter. Cameron was refusing to let them have English supplies if they signed the American Treaty Paper; and there seemed to be no other place to look for help except the Americans.

At the same time the Americans were at a big disadvantage. To persuade the Indians to sign the Treaty they promised supplies they could not, or did not, deliver. Virginia sent a trickle, far from sufficient; North Carolina sent none. The Cherokee eventually had to turn back to the British to survive. Thomas Jefferson summed up the situation two or three years later with this comment: "Their distress was too great and allowed to continue too long. It was natural that it developed into a head when we did nothing to help their needs."

The Cherokee Nation never fully recovered from this four-state invasion and destruction of their towns. The decline of their strength and capabilities gradually became more apparent in all four sections of the Nation.

A unique situation attended the July 4, 1777, session of the Cherokee-American Treaty Meet at Long Island. This day marked the first July 4th Independence Day Celebration held west of the Appalachian Mountains and, possibly, one of the first such celebrations observed in the United States. It was an odd assembly of personalities. Present were about five hundred Indians, pressured to be there by force, and two or three companies of American Militia to guard against Indian attacks. From the minutes of the Commissioners comes the following quote: "The anniversary of the Declaration of Independence was observed. The soldiers belonging to the garrison were paraded and fired two rounds; each in six platoons and for the thirteenth one general volley. The great guns were also fired."

The Indian Chiefs were made acquainted with the festivity in the following speech (and had a present of whiskey delivered to them at the same time):

> Brothers, just one year ago the thirteen United States declared themselves free and independent, and that they would no longer be in subjection and slavery to the King of Great Britain. The Americans have now for one year since their freedom fought against their enemies that came in ships over the great water, and have beat them in many battles; have killed some thousands of them and taken many prisoners, and the Great Being above hath made them very prosperous. We hope, therefore, that this day and every day hereafter will be a day of rejoicing and gladness. Brother, as this day of general rejoicing throughout the thirteen united colonies from Canada to the Floridas, we hope our brothers, the Cherokee, will now rejoice and be merry with us.

Young Indian braves who were present closed the celebration with an Indian dance. Judge Williams says that no counterpart of this celebration can be found in American history.

After the Meet was concluded, the North Carolina Commissioners made arrangements with James Robertson to act as their agent in dealing with the Cherokee. Virginia made similar arrangements with Joseph Martin to serve as Virginia's representative in handling Indian affairs.

This was Joseph Martin's formal entry into the Cherokee story. Commissioned by Governor Patrick Henry as Agent and Superintendent of Indian Affairs for the State of Virginia, November 3, 1777, he continued in this position until 1789. As Superintendent, he took up residence at the famous rendezvous of the Territory, Long Island, on the Holston. He built a store house on the Island for the purpose of depositing such goods as the Government might send out for the Indians. William Martin, son of Joseph, told Draper: "When he (Joseph Martin) was appointed Agent to the Cherokee, he took a young half-breed Cherokee, by the name of Betsy Ward, to wife. She was of the most distinguished clan of the whole tribe, and one of the finest families of that clan." Betsy (Elizabeth) Ward was the daughter of Nancy and Bryant Ward. From later reports, Joseph Martin maintained two residences — one at Long Island and another at Chota. William Martin says Betsy spent much of her married life with Martin at Long Island.

THE CHICKAMAUGA RAID

The year of the three sevens (1777) has been referred to as *The Bloody Year* by Kentucky historians. The Chickamaugans, dissident Creeks, and Shawnee war parties kept the southwest Virginians and Kentucky frontier families inside forts much of that year; and this continued harassment brought about some daring planning by the Virginians and North Carolinians.

During this period of quiet between the Watauga and the Overhill Settlements, trails across the mountains were filled with movers headed toward the promised land. All elements of humankind were among this horde of newcomers: good, bad, Rebels, Tories, and Indian haters. Indian boundary lines were ignored as this rash of comers squatted on settlement fringes and staked their claims.

Joseph Martin, who had been appointed Virginia's agent to the Cherokee, took up his duties during November 1777. Martin built a storehouse on Long Island to keep whatever supplies the officials of the two states might send in for the Indians. James Robertson, appointed as North Carolina's agent at about the same time, had moved to the mouth of Big Creek near present Rogersville, Tennessee.

During the years 1777-1778, Henry Hamilton, Lieutenant-Governor of Canada and the Northwest Territory, was stirring up Indian troubles in that section of the country. Hamilton was trying to win the cooperation of all the eastern tribes from north to south to be ready to attack the backside of the colonies when another British coastal assault was attempted. Hamilton, called the *Hair Buyer*, had many conferences with allied Chiefs including Dragging Canoe. The Canoe's reputation as a strong warrior Chief had spread among most of the eastern tribes. Hamilton was planning to use the Chickamauga warriors to hit the southern colonies when the time was right. In preparation for this, three hundred pack-horse-loads of ammunition, guns, and other supples had been hauled in and stored at John McDonald's home near Look Out Mountain (Chattanooga, Tennessee).

Plans were also being made by Virginia's Governor, Patrick Henry, and Colonel George Rogers Clark that would upset Hamilton's grandiose scheme. Colonel Clark, with a rather small force, invaded the Northwest Territory and captured Kaskaskia July 4, 1778, without bloodshed. Shortly afterward, Vincennes was occupied in the same manner. In December 1778, Governor Hamilton was able to retake Vincennes, where he stored a large stock of ammunition and other supplies to be issued the Indians. On February 22, 1779, Clarke again took Vincennes, along with all the stored supplies, and captured Hamilton the scalp buyer himself, who was delivered as prisoner to the Virginia authorities.

Another campaign of equal importance which would further upset Dragging Canoe's grand hopes was being put together by the Virginia-Carolina officials. James Robertson, North Carolina's agent to the Cherokee, had returned from Chota during September of 1778 with a report that the Overhill towns were friendly, but no lasting peace seemed possible with the Chickamaugans. Joseph Martin, Virginia's agent, reported about the same thing to Virginia authorities. Martin advised an early attack on the Chickamauga settlements.

Both states decided to move against Dragging Canoe as quickly as preparations could be made. Money was appropriated to pay the expenses; and various companies were instructed to rendezvous at James Robertson's fort at the mouth of Big Creek on the Holston the first of April, 1779. Colonel John Montgomery, who was in the area enlisting volunteers to reinforce Colonel Clark in the Northwest, was commandeered along with his men.

Colonel Evan Shelby was placed in charge of the expedition. A conference with his fellow officers resulted in plans to make the trip downriver by boats; and Isaac Shelby was placed in charge of preparing enough dugout canoes to accommodate the six-hundred-man force. With broad axes and adzes, tall poplar trees were downed; and soon, sufficient long boats and piroques were ready for the trip.

This frontier force left Big Creek about April 10, 1779. April rains had flushed the river, so the speedy current made for a fast trip downstream. Shelby's force reached the mouth of Chickamauga Creek five days later.

The unexpected approach by water caught the Chickamaugans off guard. A lone Indian fisherman, captured near the mouth of the creek, was forced to lead the Americans to the Indian towns. Dragging Canoe's warriors were barely able to put up enough resistance to give their women and children time to escape into the hills before retreating themselves.

Shelby and his men spent about two weeks in the Chickamauga settlements. They burned and destroyed about eleven towns. As crops had not been planted, there were none to destroy. The frontiersmen did appropriate the corn and potatoes found, for their own use. The three hundred pack-horse-loads of supplies stored at John McDonald's were captured along with a big cache of furs.

Mission completed, Shelby's force departed. They crossed the river to where their boats were docked and headed back

An authentic two-hundred-year-old Cherokee dugout canoe, twenty-two feet long, discovered in the Chatahoochie River, North Georgia, in 1974 by Delbert Greer, has been donated to the Museum of the Cherokee Indian in Cherokee, North Carolina. The Greer family assisted Dr. and Mrs. Duane King, the Cherokee Oral History Club, Thomas Buetell of Tuckasegee, and others to transport the canoe to Cherokee where it is undergoing chemical preservation treatment to prepare it for exhibition at the Cherokee museum.
(Photo courtesy Dr. Duane King, Dirctor of Museum.)

upstream. Paddling and poling upriver made for slow progress, so they decided it would be easier to make the return trip on foot. They destroyed all the boats except those needed by Colonel Montgomery and his men to continue on toward the northwest to join Colonel Clark.

Colonel Shelby held a public auction upriver near the mouth of a small stream. The purpose was to dispose of the supplies captured at McDonald's and to sell the captured horses. Shelby himself bid off one of the animals. The creek where the auction was held has been called *Sale Creek* since that day.

The destruction of his towns was a severe blow to Dragging Canoe, but he was not ready to "call it quits." His manpower loss was small, and they could get more supplies from the English. In order to avoid a repetition of the attack by water, the Chickamaugans moved around the base of Look Out Mountain and settled below the breaks where the boiling pot, *suck or whirl*, made the river difficult to navigate. A few warriors on constant guard could easily defend their new settlements.

DISASTER STRIKES AGAIN

Several events occurred during the year 1779 that spelled more trouble and brought additional problems to the Cherokee. One was the appointment of John Sevier as Colonel of the Washington County (Tennessee) Militia. Another was the establishment of the Cumberland Settlements in Middle Tennessee. A third was the beginning of an almost successful conquest of the South by British forces under Cornwallis.

As Colonel of the frontier militia, John Sevier was both judge and jury in deciding when he thought the Indians needed chastising. If he thought the need was sufficient, he summoned his men and hit the war trail. John Sevier was destined to ride the Indian War Path to fame during the 1780 decade.

James Robertson and John Donelson persuaded a party of settlers to go with them to French Lick (Nashville, Tennessee) and establish a new settlement. Robertson led the land party over the Wilderness Trail through Cumberland Gap and present Kentucky. Driving their stock, brood mares, and loaded pack horses to French Lick, they arrived around Christmas of 1779 and established Nashborough. John Donelson, leading a flotilla of some thirty boats, took the women, children, and household furnishings down the river route. After a venturesome, perilous trip, they arrived at Nashborough April 24, 1780. These two related events signaled the real beginning of the Cumberland Settlements.

Lord Clinton was able to enter through the Savannah, Georgia, port and begin the almost successful British invasion of the South. Colonel Campbell, with 3,000 troops, soon had Georgia under British control and moved on into South Carolina. Charleston was forced to surrender May 12, 1780, when Clinton laid siege with a coastal assault. Clinton placed General Cornwallis in charge of the southern campaign. With Colonel Banastre Tarlton and his merciless dragoons to strike terror in the settlements, and Colonel Patrick Ferguson with a strong enough force of Tories to sweep the western sectors of the two Carolinas, the South was nearly licked. The main British Army was encamped at Charlotte, North Carolina, and since no resistance was evident ahead, North Carolina and Virginia seemed doomed.

Colonel Ferguson's successful sweep through the western sectors of the two Carolinas caused him to make his big mistake. Irritated by the hit-and-run sorties of the Overmountain Men during several South Carolina engagements, Colonel Ferguson sent a threatening letter to Colonel Isaac Shelby which included other western officers. This threat brought an unknown army of backwoodsmen across the mountains who followed Ferguson to King's Mountain and completely annihilated his well-equipped force. Colonel Ferguson himself was killed. The mountaineer army used tactics learned from the Indians in this incredible battle. The victory spelled disaster to the British cause in the South and further doomed the Indians.

The successful conquest by the British in Georgia and South Carolina had again established convenient supply lines for the southern Indians. They flocked to the supply depot in Augusta, Georgia, in large numbers. To get the desperately needed English supplies, however, they had to pay a price. Colonel Thomas Brown, who had succeeded Captain John Stuart as English Indian Agent in the South, sent the following letter to Lord Cornwallis from Augusta:

> In consequence of letters sent to the Cherokee Nation, the Indians have agreed to attack Rebel Plunderers who have taken possession of their hunting grounds on the Watauga. Chiefs of 2,500 Cherokee warriors promise to continue the war during the winter if they are provided with arms and ammunition and their families are provided with clothing. No towns remaining friendly with the Rebels will receive any supplies.

Colonel Brown was also aware of Joseph Martin's strong anti-British influence in the Overhill towns; and he instructed John McDonald, British Agent in Chickamauga, to do something about the matter. McDonald appeared in Chota and attempted to arrest Martin; but Oconostota, Hanging Maw, and Nancy Ward were powerful enough to protect their friend. Joseph Martin had been exerting his influence in the Cherokee Council in efforts to persuade the Overhill Indians to stay out of this war. It was an impossible mission because during the Long Island Treaty of July 1777, the Virginia-North Carolina officials had promised supplies they evidently could not, or did not deliver. The situation had continued to such an extent that when the greatly needed British supplies became available, Cherokee warriors became British Allies in fact and deed. Overhill warriors "took Dragging Canoe by the arm" and joined in the war.

When the Overmountain Men mustered at Sycamore Shoals September 25, 1780, to cross the mountains and do battle with Ferguson, British Agents told the Indians, "Now is the time to get your land back. All the men of the Watauga and Nolichucky will be gone and no one will be left to fight except old men and young boys. The King's soldiers will soon kill off those untrained backwoodsmen who have crossed the mountains."

The King's Mountain Battle was over and the fighters back home before the Indians had really made a good start on the warparth. The result of the King's Mountain Battle was far different from British predictions. The Overmountain Men, who had learned the art of guerilla fighting from the Indians, had fooled the experts.

Nancy Ward again entered the picture as a peace mediator when she sent a warning of the oncoming Indian attacks to John Sevier. Oconostota, Old Tassel, Hanging Maw, and Nancy Ward had strongly opposed the warring faction of Chiefs in this new campaign to attack the settlements. These older Headmen had only too recently experienced the tragedies wrought on their Nation by white armies, and neither could Nancy relish a war waged on old people, women, and children. Perhaps she hoped by sending this warning that much bloodshed could be avoided.

The three traders taking Nancy's message to the settlements were Isaac Thomas, Ellis Harlan, and Henry (William) Springstone. An interesting item about the three messengers is related by Hale and Merritt (two historians) who suggest that, for obvious reasons, Isaac

Thomas has been suspected of being Nancy's paramour during those troubled years. They point out that he was young and possessed of the qualities that appealed strongly to her sex. Ellis Harlan was then or later became the third husband of Catherine, daughter of Nancy and Kingfisher. Henry Springstone was a close friend and worked with Joseph Martin, Nancy Ward's son-in-law.

John Sevier found Isaac Thomas and Ellis Harlan waiting at his home when he returned from King's Mountain. Overmountain officials had been anticipating such an attack so Nancy's warning served to speed up plans for immediate action. Sevier wanted to stop the warriors before they reached the Nolichucky valley settlements. Henry Springstone had gone on to Long Island to make his report to Joseph Martin.

Colonel Sevier immediately dispatched riders to summon his men to meet him at Swan Pond on Lick Creek. Instead of going to Long Island to confer with Colonel Arthur Campbell and Major Joseph Martin, Sevier sent a message to Major Martin advising him of his intention to march at once against the Indians.

The third night after leaving the Lick Creek Camp, Sevier's force of 300 men made camp at Boyd's Creek (Sevier County, Tennessee). Early morning scouting discovered the Indian force encamped within three miles of their own camp. The Indians had not expected to see such a large force of fighting men because they thought the patriots were across the mountains fighting the British soldiers. Following is a descriptive narrative of the Boyd Creek Battle as taken from Ramsey:

> The Indians had formed in a half moon, and lay concealed in the grass. Had their stratagem not been discovered, their position, and shape of the ground, would have enabled them to enclose and overcome the horsemen. Lieutenant Lane and John Ward had dismounted for the fight, when Sevier, having noticed the semicircular position of the Indians, ordered a halt, with the purpose of engaging the top extremes of the Indian line, and keeping up the action until the other part of his troops could come up. Lane and his comrade, Ward, remounted and fell back upon Sevier without being hurt, though fired at by several warriors near them. A brief fire was, for a short time, kept up by Sevier's Party and the nearest Indians. The troops behind, hearing the first fire, had quickened their pace and were coming in sight. James Roddy, with about twenty men, quickly came up, and soon after the main body of the troops. The Indians noticed the reinforcements and closed their lines. Sevier immediately ordered the charge, which would have been still more fatal, but that the pursuit led through a swampy branch, which impeded the progress of the horsemen.

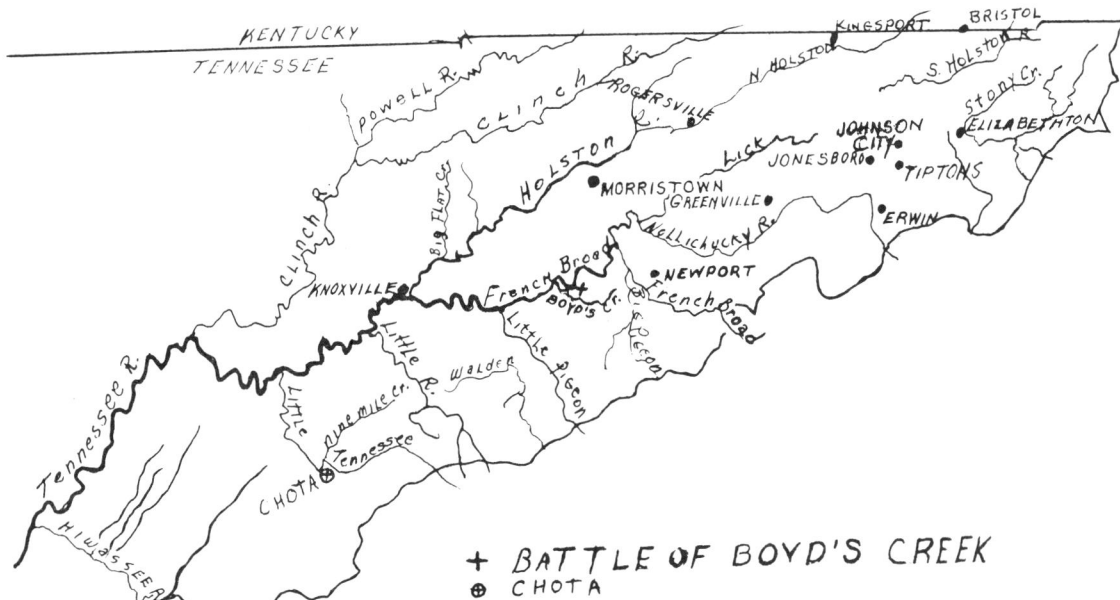

+ BATTLE OF BOYD'S CREEK
⊕ CHOTA

Just as the successful Boyd Creek engagement was ending, two men, Old French Frank and Henry Springstone, arrived at Sevier's camp with a message from Colonel Arthur Campbell asking Sevier to await his (Campbell's) arrival before proceeding to the Cherokee towns.

Colonel Sevier pulled his men back about eight miles and set up camp. After a week had passed and food supplies were exhausted, Sevier's force moved back to the Boyd Creek area hoping to find some wild game. Wildlife was so scarce the men had to depend on meager findings of dried grapes, haws, roots, hickory nuts, and walnuts to survive. Colonel Campbell and his command did not arrive at Sevier's camp until December 22, 1780, nearly two weeks after Sevier's fight with the Indians. Campbell divided his small supply of corn with the hungry men. They parched this and made out as they continued their march.

The Overmountain Men's army reached Chota Christmas Eve, finding the Cherokee capital abandoned, as were other Overhill towns. The unexpected approach of so large a white army caused the Overhill Indians to flee to the hills for safety. Campbell's army spent Christmas Eve killing hogs and poultry left behind by the Cherokee; then most of Christmas night was spent cooking and eating the Indians' food.

Following are excerpts from Colonel Arthur Campbell's official report to Virginia's Governor Thomas Jefferson, dated January 15, 1781. (The full report can be found in Virginia's Calendar of State Papers.)

> The 22nd [December 22, 1780] — I crossed the French River and found the Wattago men in great want of provisions. We gave them a supply from our small stock, and the next day made a forced march toward the Tenasee. The success of the enterprise seemed to rest on our safely reaching the further bank of that river, as we had information the Indians had obstructed the common fording places, and had a force ready there to oppose our crossing. The morning of the 24th I made a feint towards the island town, or Dragging Canoe's town, the lowermost on the river, and with the main body passed the river without resistance at Timotlee.
>
> We were now discovered. Such of the Indians we saw seemed to be flying in consternation. Here I divided my force, sending a part to attack the towns below, and with the other, I proceeded towards their principal town, Chote. Just as I passed a defile above Toque, I observed the Indians in force, stretching along the hills below Chote, with an apparent design to attack our Van then within their view; but the main body too soon came in sight for me to succeed in decoying them off the hills; so they quietly let us pass on in order, without firing a gun, except a few scattering shots at our rear, at a distance from the clefts. We soon were in possession of their beloved town [Chota], in which we found a welcome supply of provisions.
>
> By the returns of the officers of different detachments, we killed 29 men and took 17 prisoners, mostly women and children. The number of wounded is uncertain. Besides these we brought in the family of Nancy Ward, who for their good offices, we considered in another light. The whole are in Major Martin's care at the Great Island, until the sense of government is known how they are to be disposed of.
>
> The towns of Chote, Scittigo, (?), Chilhowee, Toque, Mieliqua, Kai-a-tee, Sattooga, Telico, Hiwasee and Chistowee, all principal towns, besides some small ones and several scattering settlements, in which were upwards of 1,000 houses, and not less than 50,000 bushels of corn, and large quantities of other kinds of provisions, all of which, after taking sufficient subsistance for the army whilest in the country and on its return, were committed to flames, or otherwise destroyed. No place in the Over H[ill] country remained unvisited, except the small town of Telasee, a scattering settlement, in the neighborhood of Chickamogga, and the town of Caloogee situated on the sources of the Mobile.

At Chota, Nancy Ward had a small herd of cattle driven in to furnish meat for the troops. Colonel Elijah Clark, with Sevier's command, had his men slaughter the cattle and dress the meat ready for use. On discovering this, Colonel Joseph Martin rescued the meat by force. A fist fight between Martin and Clarke followed. This altercation caused a rift between Martin's followers and Sevier's men that lasted many years. It has been assumed that Joseph Martin had made the arrangements with Nancy for the cattle. The certificate mentioned in the following letter is thought to be payment to Nancy Ward for the cattle.

TO MAJ. JOSEPH MARTIN   Jan. 14, 1781

Dear Sir: I received yours of the 12th. According to your request, have sent Nancy Ward the certificate. I thank you for your kind offer to serve me in carrying down any demands of mine. I have got a person to take down some letters. Am glad you are agoing down, as you can inform them fully of any particular circumstances relating our campaign. I am, sir, with esteem and your most obedient servant,

MS:Draper11DD93.   John Sevier

Another part of Campbell's report says:

    That famous Indian Woman Nancy Ward came to camp; she gave us various intelligence and made an overture in behalf of some of the chiefs for peace, to which I avoided giving an explicit answer, as I wished first to visit the vindictive part of the nation, mostly settled at Hiwassee and Chestowee, and to distress the whole as much as possible by destroying their habitations and provisions.

It is said Nancy Ward had asked Colonel Campbell to spare Hiwassee and Chestue. From A.V. Goodpasture comes this quote:

    Nancy Ward had a son by Kingfisher called *Little Fellow* and a brother called *Long Fellow* (Tuskegechee) who were influential chiefs. Long Fellow, Nancy's brother, boasted that he commanded seven towns, while thirteen others listened to his talks; and though he had once loved war and lived at Chickamauga, at the request of his nephew, General Joseph Martin, he had moved to Chestue, midway between Chota and Chickamauga [and near Hiwassee], where he stood like a wall between bad people and his brothers the Virginians.

BATTLE OF THE HORSES AND HOUNDS

The campaign against the Cherokee in December 1780, by the Overmountain Men of the Holston, Watauga, and Nolichucky settlements, was led by Colonel John Sevier, Major Joseph Martin, and Colonel Arthur Campbell. Even though many towns were burned and treaty terms agreed on, this left untouched the main source of the Cumberland Indian troubles. The Chickamauga Nation was made up of dissident Cherokee who broke away from the Overhill Towns and formed a Nation of their own. Many Creeks from north Georgia and the Alabama territory had joined the Chickamauga warriors.

Unable to do much against the stronger settlements of the Holston, Watauga, and Nolichucky, Dragging Canoe decided to move against the young, weaker settlements in the Cumberland basin. He wanted to wipe them out before they had time to grow strong. So, in March of 1781, he left Chickamauga leading a strong force of several hundred. His first attack was to be against Nashborough at French Lick. When he had overcome and destroyed the main stronghold of the whites, the others would fall easily. Plans and details for the attack were worked out carefully; and the various bands of warriors were able to move into the settlements without any problem. As the settlers had not anticipated an attack of this magnitude, Dragging Canoe's plan was working better than he had hoped.

During the night of April 1st, Dragging Canoe arranged his forces in pre-battle positions, and they moved into strategic places for an all-out assault. James Menefee, standing watch, fired a shot during the night at an Indian scout. This was not an unusual occurrence, so the hemmed and herded people asleep inside the stockade were not alarmed. They had little inkling of what was taking place outside the fort.

Early dawn April 2nd, the sentry cry of "Indians" aroused the people. Three braves had approached the fort, fired their guns, and run back out of gun range. They stopped, reloaded, and went through a lot of antics to attract attention. The men in the fort felt this was a ruse to draw them outside; but the decision was made to go after them. James Robertson left the fort with a force of twenty men, planning to run them down; and at full gallop they took off after the warriors. The Indians running away from the fort were soon joined by another group; and they stopped to make a stand. Arriving within firing distance, Robertson and his men dismounted and prepared to fight. About this time, another large band of Indians, concealed in the bed of a creek, rushed out behind the whites and began firing on the frontiersmen from the rear. The twenty guns of the whites returned the fire with good effect. This crossfire and the loud whoops of the redskins so frightened the horses that they stampeded back toward the fort. Now another large body of Indians that had been concealed in the cedars ran out to join in the fray. Their lines extended back toward the fort; but the frantic horses broke through both lines in their mad panic.

The sight of those twenty beautiful horses caused many of the Indians to forget the battle in progress and chase the animals — horses were prized about as much as scalps. By this time the large force stationed beyond the fort sallied out to come between the men and the fort gate. This band of Indians was the one designated to enter the stockade. The horses breaking through the Indian lines made an opening, through which the twenty men were trying to fight their way toward the gate. This advantage was greatly strengthened by so many of the warriors chasing after the horses, which had swerved away from the fort in their mad effort to escape this new menace of whooping warriors.

All of the fighting and commotion of the battle raging outside was being watched by the people inside. The women, with axes and loaded guns in hand, were determined to sell their lives dearly. Mrs. James Robertson had gone to the wall overlooking the area where the twenty men were fighting; and she saw the horses break through the Indian lines, followed by a host of warriors. She watched her husband and his men desperately fighting their way toward the fort through the broken Indian lines. The whining and wailing of the Indian-hating dogs, penned in the fort, gave her the great inspiration. Going to the guard at the gate, she told him to open it and let the dogs out. With savage fury this reserve army of Nashborough rushed into the fray; and the Indians became so excited with this unexpected attack, they almost forgot the pioneers. The red warriors were kept busy defending themselves from the vicious attacks of the more than fifty dogs. They did not want to waste shots on the animals, and anyway it was next to impossible to hit the whirling, snarling, biting beasts.

In the conflict known as the Battle of the Bluffs it was the Indians' love of horses and fear of hounds that made the difference. (Illustration by Bernie Andrews used by courtesy of Mary U. Rothrock, author of *This is Tennessee.***)**

The confusion, caused by some of the Indians chasing horses and others fighting off the vicious dogs, gave the pioneers a chance to gain the fort gate. Five men were killed: Alexander Buchanan, George Kennedy, Zachariah White, Peter Gill, and Captain Leiper. James Menefee, Joseph Moonshaw and Isaac Lucas were wounded. During the final desperate run for the fort, Lucas was shot and his hip was broken. Lying in the ground, he reloaded his gun and shot the front Indian of the pursuing group before being rescued. Another struggle took place within yards of the fort wall. Edward Swanson was overtaken by a big buck Indian who hit him with the butt of his gun, causing Swanson to drop his own rifle. Swanson turned and grabbed the Indian's gun in an effort to wrest it away from the red man. It was a life and death struggle, which the Indian seemed to be winning. Getting complete possession of his gun, the big buck knocked Swanson to his knees and was in the act of finishing him off when his own gun refused to fire. At this point, John Buchanan, who had nearly reached the gate, shot the Indian and helped Swanson to safety.

As the men reached the protection of the fort walls, they were able to give the Indians some deadly fire; and about ten o'clock the Indians withdrew out of gun range. The Battle of the Bluffs was really the Battle of the Horses and Hounds. The Indians' lack of discipline, at the critical moment, lost the victory already won. The demoralized Indians continued to chase the horses, and caught some of the animals with the saddles and gear still intact. Some of the horses eluded the warriors and returned to the fort gates, which were opened for them to pass inside.

A close watch was kept throughout the day, though the Indians had pulled back out of gun range to plan their next move. That night they began firing at the fort. This continued for some time, but very little damage was done. The lookouts noticed a band of several hundred Indians assembled in an area beyond rifle range; and it was decided to fire the small swivel cannon at this body of warriors. They collected scraps of iron and broken stones to use in place of regular cannonballs. Each man gave a charge from his own powder horn to supply the load, though many protested because of the scarcity of powder. The gun was placed in position and aimed at the large group. Its boom was worse than its bite, but the loud bang of the explosion frightened the Indians. These warriors also knew that men from the other stations would be coming to the aid of the besieged fort. The Indian force left.

NANCY WARD, CHIEFTAINESS

Before leaving the Overhill country, Colonel Arthur Campbell and the other officers sent an ultimatum to the Cherokee Chiefs and their warriors. The message demanded that within two moons six of their Headmen report to Joseph Martin (Indian Agent for both Virginia and North Carolina) at Long Island to arrange a treaty. If they didn't cooperate, the army would further lay waste to their country.

Nancy Ward and members of her family were taken back to Long Island (on the Holston River, Kingsport, Tennessee) by her son-in-law. Betsy, Nancy's daughter and Indian wife of Joseph Martin, was living there at the time.

When General Nathaniel Greene received Campbell's report of the campaign against the Cherokee and notice of the proposed treaty, he sent messages from his camp in North Carolina to William Preston, William Christain, Arthur Campbell, and Joseph Martin of Virginia. The same messages were sent to Evan Shelby, Joseph Williams, and John Sevier of North Carolina. These men were empowered to form a commission to treat with the Cherokee Chiefs for peace, exchange prisoners, and adjust boundaries. Any five of the above-named commission were authorized to act during the Treaty Meet to be held on Long Island; however, the Continental Congress must approve any treaty negotiated at this Meet. Greene's instructions also stated: "The Cherokee were to appoint delegates to meet with Congress for the purpose of obtaining such enlargements of confirmation of their treaties as may appear to them requisite."

The Nolichucky, Watauga, and Holston people were not pleased with the "any enlargements" phrase; and they liked even less Greene's following statement: "You are hereby charged to call on the commanding officers of the adjacent counties for force and assistance to prevent further encroachment by subjects of the United States on the lands of the Tribes of Indian Nations." This statement sounded great to the Indians; but the insatiable lust of the whites for the red man's land filled the words with empty meaning.

The Long Island Treaty Meet finally got started July 26, 1781. The Commissioners reminded the attending Chiefs "... that their British Allies could no longer furnish them aid, as they had been suppressed in battle; thus the Cherokee must look to the Americans for any help or cooperation they might receive."

The Carpenter was now dead and Oconostota very old. Kaiyah-tahee (Old Tassel) had been asked by Oconostota to take charge of the Meet for the Council. The Tassel began by blaming their troubles on Colonel Brown, Cameron, and Dragging Canoe, saying, "We were opposed to this war and tried to restrain the young Chiefs but they would not listen." Turning to Colonel John Seivier, Chief Tassel said, "I know that you are a man and a warrior. I have heard different talks by different people quite different from what I expected. I fear you must have been angry and that it was caused by some evil persons. . . . You have risen up from a warrior to a Beloved Man. I hope your speech will be good." John Sevier replied that he had never hated the Cherokee, but had fought them for the safety of his people. (The Chief and Sevier most likely were referring to Sevier's recent attack on Middle Towns located on the Tuckasegee River in North Carolina during March of 1781.)

At this point in the proceedings, an event occurred that has no historical parallel. An Indian woman rose from her seat among the group of attending Cherokee women and approached the Treaty negotiators. This was no ordinary woman; this was Nancy Ward, Cherokee Woman Chieftainess. She spoke:

> **You know that women are always looked upon as nothing; but we are your mothers; you are our sons. OUR CRY IS ALL FOR PEACE; let it continue. This peace must last forever. Let your women's sons be ours; our sons be yours. Let your women hear our words.**

It is said that Nancy's talk was made with the pathos, dignity and grace of her deceased uncle and mentor, Attakullakulla. The sincerity and appeal of her words reached the hearts of her listeners. Colonel William Christain, who had spared Chota in 1776, was chosen to answer Nancy's talk.

> **Mothers: we have listened well to your talk; it is humane.... No man can hear it without being moved by it. Such words and thoughts show the world that human nature is the same everywhere. Our women shall hear your words, and we know how they will feel and think of them. We are all descendants of the same woman. We will not quarrel with you because you are our mothers. We will not meddle with your people if they will be still and quiet at home and let us live in peace.**

This is one of the very few Cherokee-White peace treaties (if not the only one) when no demands were made for Indian territory. Before the Meet began, the commissioners had planned to seek all the land north of the Little Tennessee River.

Nancy Ward has been called *Great, The Pocahontas of the West,* that *Famous Indian Woman, The Cherokee Woman Chieftainess, Princess and Prophetess,* and referred to as *that beautiful, winsome, and resourceful woman, Nancy Ward.* Her talk before the commissioners is one of the classics of Cherokee literature and placed Nancy in the ranks of Great Women of America. One must remember the time of her talk was July 1781; the place, a conference of men at Long Island, ancient hallowed spot of the Cherokee; her commissioner audience, men who had just months past burned the homes and towns of her people along with their winter food supply. It took fortitude and character for any woman of that day to make such a talk.

The physical and moral conditions of the Overhill Cherokee during the years 1781-1782 were desperate. Many Indian families had been forced into the woods without food, clothing, and shelter, to live as they could or die. Roots, nuts, berries, and wildlife furnished some survival food. Rebuilding their towns was slow, and it took time to grow new crops. A large number of families moved away from the Overhill settlements and joined Lower Town families farther south on the Coosa River. Chota never regained any prominence in the Nation after its destruction. Most able-bodied warriors joined the Chickamaugans. A Moravian missionary visiting Chota on January 4, 1784, reported that, "there were only about thirty dwellings not including *Hot Houses* at that time and that Chota was the largest of the Indian Towns then on the Little Tennessee River."

Things were so bad in the Overhill settlement that in the fall of 1782 Joseph Martin took Nancy Ward and Oconostota back to Long Island to spend the winter. Scarcity of food and respect for Nancy, as well as friendship for the Old Chief who was now almost blind, were sufficient reasons. Draper's Manuscript records this quote from William Martin, son of Joseph: "I am of the opinion that Oconostota was one of the noblest and best of humankind. He had a powerful frame, and in his prime must have weighed more than two hundred pounds, with a head of enormous size. He was, when I saw him, very lean, stooped, and emaciated."

These two Cherokee greats, Nancy Ward and Oconostota, spent the winter of 1782-1783 in Joseph Martin's Long Island home, where Nancy's daughter, Betsy, was able to care for their needs. With the coming of spring, Oconostota asked Martin to take him home. The Old Chief must have felt that his end was near, and he wanted to spend his last days at Chota. Martin realized that the ailing Chief would be unable to make the trip on horseback, so he arranged to take the party downriver by boat. Sometime later, when the veteran Chief breathed his last breath, Martin buried the Old Chief with Christian rites, using a dugout canoe for a coffin.

Records do not say so, but one can safely assume that Nancy Ward accompanied her old friend on this last long journey home. It is recorded that Nancy was in the Overhill communities in the fall of 1783 visiting among her people. Nancy was in Coyatee when the following incident occurred, as recorded by Ramsey:

> During the infancy of the settlements on Nolichucky, corn became scarce and, availing themselves of a short suspension of hostilities, Jeremiah Jack and William

Rankin descended the river in a canoe to barter with the Indians for corn. They reached Koyatee without interruption. The warriors of that place refused to exchange or sell the corn, and manifested other signs of suspicion, if not of open enmity. They entered the canoe and lifted up some wearing apparel lying in it and which covered some rifles. This discovery increased the unwillingness of the Indians to trade, and they began to show a disposition to offer violence to their visitants. The Beloved Woman, Nancy Ward, happily was present, and was able by her commanding influence to appease their wrath and bring about a friendlier feeling between the parties. Little Indians were soon clad in home-made vestments brought by the traders. The canoe was filled with corn, and the white men started on their return voyage well pleased with the exchange they had made, and especially with the kind offices of the Beloved Woman.

Chota lost its greatness as the Nation's Capital center. Legend says that Nancy Ward did open her home in Chota to orphaned Indian children — mostly outcast, abandoned half-breed waifs of white traders and Indian women — providing a real sanctuary for these youngsters.

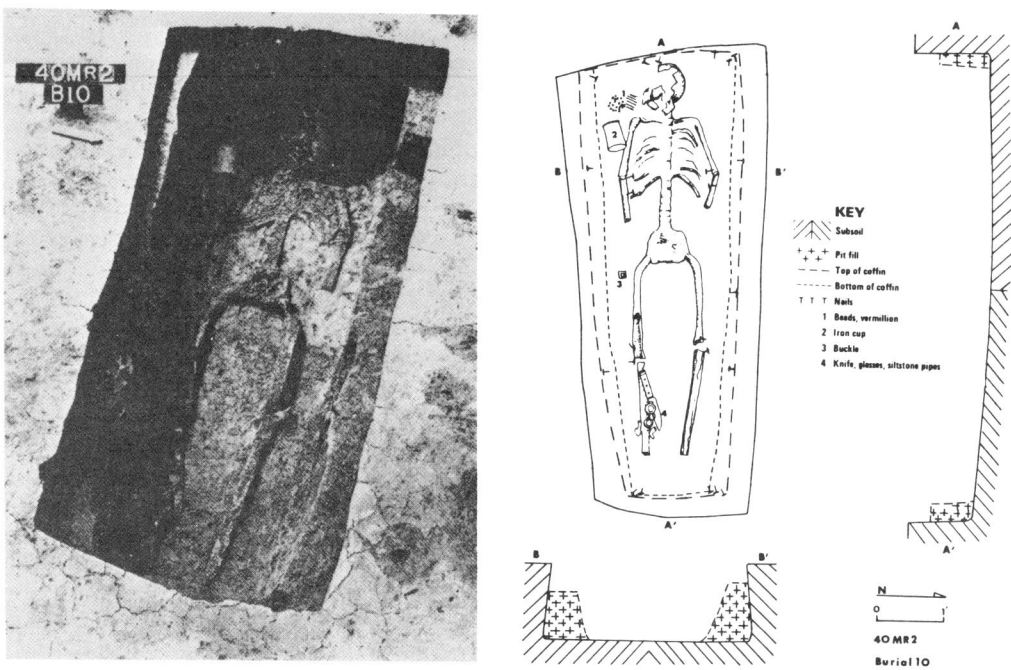

Oconostota was buried in a coffin made from a dugout canoe. The photograph on right, of Burial, was taken after excavation at Chota; drawing on left shows details of grave and location of burial accompaniments. The archaeologist's conslusion states: although there is no unequivocal proof that the burial in question is that of Oconostota, there is close correlation between archaeological and historical data. The location is right and the burial accompaniments are relative. (Photograph and drawing courtesy Duane H. King and Danny E. Olinger, "Oconostota" from *American Antiquity*, journal of the Society for American Archaeology.

CHEROKEE PAWNS

The spirit of the Cherokee people was at a low ebb. The deaths of Attakullakulla and Oconostota were like time markers in the Nation's decline. Nancy Ward endeavored to carry on the diplomatic work started by her uncle, but the task was difficult. She had strong influence among her people and the backing of the ruling Chiefs, but the virile families of the Overhill settlements and other segments of the Nation were moving to safer locations. On the other hand, the Chickamauga Settlements under Dragging Canoe's leadership were growing stronger daily. Food and clothing, as well as ammunition, were obtainable there; so deserting Cherokee, dissident Creeks, and refugee Tories were moving to Chickamauga.

The Paris Peace Treaty of 1783 formally ended the Revolutionary War; but the fighting between the frontiersmen and the red men was to continue past another decade. Spain had taken possession of the Florida Coastal Settlements and extended her holdings to New Orleans. The Mississippi River was generally considered by the colonies as their western boundary; and for years the 31st parallel was the disputed southern boundary between Spanish territory and the United States border. Spain was to enter the picture as a supplier of guns, ammunition, and lead to the southern Indians.

Along with other Overhill Chiefs, Old Tassel (now Principal Chief) had attempted to restrain the people in the upper towns from hostile acts. The situation became so desperate, with borderers and encroachers daily penetrating Indian lands below the French Broad and into the valley of the Big Pigeon, that Old Tassel wrote Carolina's Governor Martin the following letter:

> Your people from Nolichucky are daily pushing us out of our lands. We have no place to hunt on. Your people have built houses within one day's walk of our towns. We don't want to quarrel... we... hope our elder brother will not take our lands from us... because he is stronger than we are. We are the first people that ever lived on this land; it is ours and why will our elder brother take it from us?... We have done nothing to offend our elder brother since the last treaty.... We hope that... you will take pity on us your younger brother, and send Colonel Sevier, a good man, to have all your people moved off our land.

Governor Martin ordered Colonel Sevier to warn trespassers to stay off Indian land, and use force if necessary. John Sevier, closely allied with pioneer interests, simply ignored the Governor's orders.

North Carolina ceded the Southwest Territory (now Tennessee) to Congress in June 1784, after they had already disposed of most of the best land. North Carolina based its right to sell the ceded Cherokee land on the *State's Right Doctrine* that England had ceded Cherokee Land Rights to North Carolina when the treaty ending the war was signed in Paris in 1783.

When the Overmountain Settlements heard that their territory had been ceded to Congress, they met and organized their own State of Franklin. This new State functioned for approximately four years, with John Sevier as Governor. The Franklinites felt that they could use the Cherokee land, in what is now East Tennessee, to support their new government; but North Carolina repealed the cession act and tried to maintain political control over the same Southwest Territory. The Federal Government attempted the role of mediator, adding to the confusion; and the Cherokee Indians were caught in the middle of a political chess game.

Spanish authorities attempted to organize the southern tribes into a federation to fight the settlements west of the mountains. Jealous of their control over the Mississippi River basin, they offered the Indians arms and ammunition to continue their warfare against the frontiersmen.

HOPEWELL TREATY

Congress was making an effort to establish peaceful relations with the Indians. Conflicting claims of the Cherokee and the frontiersmen in the southern region was one of the main trouble spots. Without consulting Franklin officials or Cumberland leaders, arrangements were made for talks with the Cherokee; and Hopewell, South Carolina, on the Keowee River, was selected as the meeting place. Congress appointed Benjamin Hawkins, Joseph Martin, Andrew Pickens, and Lachlan McIntosh as commissioners.

The meet began November 18, 1785, with thirty-six Chiefs and almost a thousand Cherokee in attendance. The Chiefs were hopeful the new government would give them justice and fair treatment in this first Federal-Indian conference; and the Cherokee acknowledged the supremacy of the United States for the first time. The commission disavowed all previous treaties, such as Dumplin Creek, and promised the return of much of the disputed land. The agreed boundary lines left Greeneville (Tennessee), as well as areas south and west of that settlement, outside the white man's domain. Here are excerpts of the talks:

> "Congress is now sovereign of all our country, which we point out for you on the map," said a commissioner. "They want none of your lands, or anything else which belongs to you. As an earnest of their regard for you, we propose to enter into a treaty perfectly equal and conformable to what we now tell you. If you have any grievances, we will hear them, and will take such measures to correct them as may be proper."

Old Tassel replied, "The land we are now on is the land we were fighting for in the late war. The Great Man above made it for us to subsist upon. The red men are the aborigines on this country. It is but a few years since the white men found it. I am of the first stock, a native of this land. The white people are now living upon it as our friends. From the beginning of the friendship between white people and red, beads have been given as confirmation of friendship, as I now give you these beads." (Here he handed the commissioners a string of white beads.) "The people of North Carolina have taken our lands without consideration, and are now making their fortunes out of them." Taking a map offered by the commissioner, Old Tassel marked the boundaries claimed by the Cherokee and continued, "In the forks of French Broad and Holston are three thousand white people on our lands. This is a favored spot, and we cannot give it up. It is within twenty-five miles of our towns. These people must be removed."

"They are too numerous, and cannot be removed," replied the commissioners. "They settled there when the Cherokees were under the protection of the King of England. You should have asked the King to remove them."

"Is not Congress, which conquered the King of England, strong enough to remove these people?" asked the Chief.

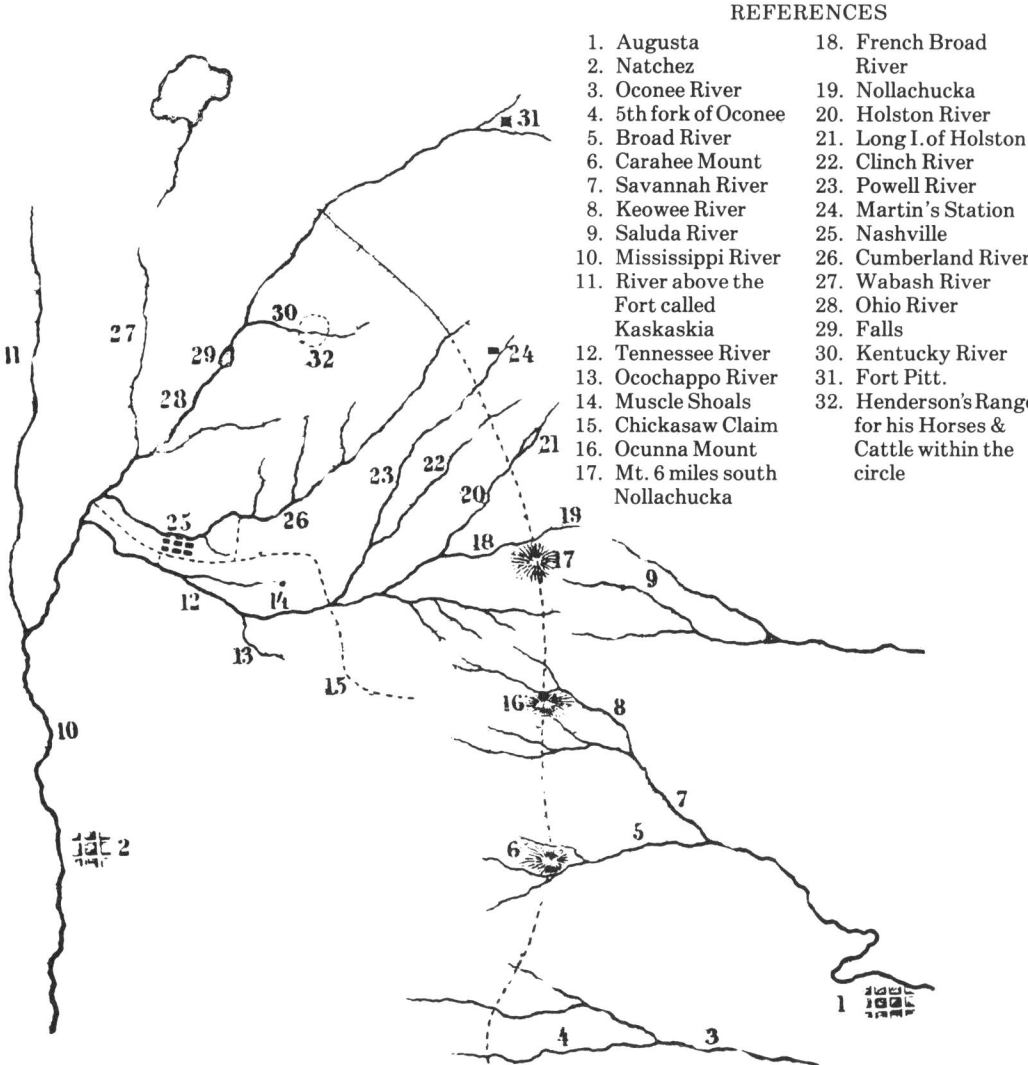

REFERENCES

1. Augusta
2. Natchez
3. Oconee River
4. 5th fork of Oconee
5. Broad River
6. Carahee Mount
7. Savannah River
8. Keowee River
9. Saluda River
10. Mississippi River
11. River above the Fort called Kaskaskia
12. Tennessee River
13. Ocochappo River
14. Muscle Shoals
15. Chickasaw Claim
16. Ocunna Mount
17. Mt. 6 miles south Nollachucka
18. French Broad River
19. Nollachucka
20. Holston River
21. Long I. of Holston
22. Clinch River
23. Powell River
24. Martin's Station
25. Nashville
26. Cumberland River
27. Wabash River
28. Ohio River
29. Falls
30. Kentucky River
31. Fort Pitt.
32. Henderson's Range for his Horses & Cattle within the circle

This map is copied from one marked by the Tassel to describe Cherokee claims presented at treaty November 1785, at Hopewell on Keowee. The dotted lines show the reduced territory now agreed upon as a dividing ridge between the Cumberland and Tennessee Rivers, forty miles above Nashville.

Old Tassel insisted that they would not give up the land but finally agreed to leave the matter to Congress. The final boundaries agreed on at Hopewell started on the Cumberland River, forty miles north of Nashville, and ran to a point six miles south of the Nolichucky and southward of Oconee River. The town of Greeneville, then Capital of the State of Franklin, had been returned to the Cherokee.

Before signing the treaty, Old Tassel requested permission for the Woman of Chota, the famous Nancy Ward, to talk to the commissioners. She said:

"I am glad there is now peace. I take you by the hand in real friendship. I have a pipe and a little tobacco to give the commissioners to smoke in friendship. I look on you and the red people as my children. Your having determined on peace is most pleasant to me for I have seen much trouble during the late war. I am old, but I hope yet to bear children, who will grow up and people our Nation, as we are now under the protection of Congress and shall have no more disturbance. The talk I have given you is from the young warriors I have raised in my town, as well as myself. They rejoice that we have peace, and hope the chain of friendship will never more be broken." Nancy delivered two strings of wampum, a pipe, and some tobacco to the white commissioners.

The last clause in the treaty stated: **"Any settler who fails to remove within six months from the land guaranteed to the Indians shall forfeit the protection of the United States, and the Cherokee may punish him or not as they please."** This Treaty brought protests from North Carolina, State of Franklin, and the Cumberland Officials. Nobody liked it. The last clause was an open invitation to the Indians to harass the five thousand settlers below this boundary line. The State of Franklin completely disregarded any part of the Hopewell Treaty.

Nancy Ward's prominence during the next few years was somewhat eclipsed by the rising star of her cousin, Dragging Canoe. He became War Chief of the Cherokee and strong man of the Nation, though his followers were called Chickamaugans.

THE TOMAHAWK STRIKES AGAIN

Congress firmly believed it had the power to force trespassers off Cherokee lands, as was promised at the Hopewell Treaty; and the Cherokee placed great faith in the Congressional guarantee to protect their interests. The Cherokee Council accepted literally the last clause of the agreement which read: "Any settler who fails to remove within six months from the land guaranteed to the Indians shall forfeit the protection of the United States, and the Cherokee may punish him or not as they please."

Federal officials made efforts to enforce the treaty but were almost powerless to keep their pledge. During the six or seven years following the Revolutionary War, the United States was more or less a loose Federation of Independent Commonwealths until the Federal Constitution was adopted by all thirteen states. Each state had retained its state rights status which could not be infringed upon, and handled its own Indian affairs — sometimes very badly. The Indians did not, and could not, understand the situation. They could only see the terms of the treaty being broken day after day.

As months passed and Congress made no visible move to stop the transgressors, the angered Indians took matters into their own hands and began raiding families who had settled on land promised them by the Federal Government. According to the treaty terms, they expected Congress to justify their actions. Instead, angered frontiersmen struck back and bloody atrocities were committed on both sides.

Space does not permit the listing of fights and massacres — by both reds and whites — during this period. Needless to say, every cabin, spring, farm, and trail was a likely scene of tragedy and death. Savage massacres were committed by red warriors, who, following centuries old customs and methods of warfare, spared neither man, woman, nor child. White frontiersmen, who had adopted Indian guerilla tactics, were just as brutal in their raids.

An unreasoning hate for Indians had developed among white frontier settlers. Many considered the aborigine natives as animals rather than humans. This attitude was somewhat summed up by one frontiersman who said to John Heckewelder, a Moravian Missionary: "An Indian has no more soul than a Buffalo. To kill either is the same thing, and when you have killed an Indian you have done a good act and have killed a wild beast."

White immigrants wanted Indian land, so they planned and connived to get it by any means possible. Judge David Campbell of Franklin State described the craze for land in this manner: "No people are entitled to more land than they can cultivate. People will not sit still and starve for land when a neighboring Nation has more than it needs."

Franklin Militia commanded by General William Cocke and Colonel Alexander Outlaw made a show of force at Coyatee, where, with threats and military pressure, they practically forced Old Tassel and Hanging Maw into surrendering the rich lands between the French Broad and Little Tennessee Rivers. The Chiefs were told: "The New State has bought all the land north of the Little Tennessee and intend to settle it, and if any Cherokee interferes his town will be burned."

Joseph Martin, Indian Agent for both North Carolina and Virginia, had repeatedly protested to the unlawful encroachers settled on Indian land; but the trespassers told Martin it was none of his business where they lived, that they were responsible to no government. Old Tassel is credited with the following quote: "We have held several treaties with the Americans when boundaries were fixed and fair promises made that the white people would not cross over, but we always find that after a treaty they settle much faster than before. Truth is if we had no land we should have fewer enemies."

One John Kirk, taking advantage of a peaceful period, built his cabin several miles south of present Knoxville, Tennessee, and moved his family there. The action angered some Cherokee warriors, who massacred eleven members of the family. The father and a son, John Jr., were absent at the time. This incident brought Colonel John Sevier and the Franklin Militia with destructive raids against upper towns of the Cherokee. As the warriors were thought to be from Chilhowie, Colonel Sevier sent Major Hubbard to destroy that town. This choice was unfortunate because Hubbard was an Indian hater, and also because John Kirk, Jr. was in Hubbard's company. Major Hubbard arranged to get Old Tassel, Hanging Maw of Chota and his brother, together with Old Abram and a son, under a flag of truce for talks. When the Chiefs were seated in the designated cabin, Major Hubbard closed the door and handed John Kirk, Jr. a tomahawk, saying: "Take the vengeance to which you are entitled." The Chiefs, realizing their betrayal, made no effort to resist. Young Kirk killed all five of the unprotesting Headmen.

This action sent almost avery able-bodied warrior in the Nation hurrying to join Dragging Canoe's war camp. Colonel John Sevier was blamed for this murder of the Chiefs, even though he was absent and later publicly deplored the incident; but Governor Johnson of North Carolina issued a warrant for his arrest on a charge of treason and wilful murder. Colonel Sevier was arrested and taken to Morganton, North Carolina; but he was never arraigned in court and soon returned home.

The killing of their Principal Chief electrified the Cherokee Nation into action. John Watts and Bench, nephews of Tassel, swore vengeance against all whites. Doublehead, Tassel's brother, and many other Chiefs began making retaliatory raids against nearby settlements. The white frontiersmen struck back with a vengeance which started an all out war.

In addition to his Indian Agent duties, Joseph Martin was also Brigadier-General of the western North Carolina forces. He was practically forced into leading a campaign against the Chickamaugans. Several of the officers and men making up Martin's command didn't like him. There was a hang-over of ill will from the friction between Sevier's followers and Martin's men which started during the Campbell-Martin-Sevier 1780-1781 campaign against the Cherokee. Many considered General Martin an Indian lover and unfriendly toward frontier expansion into Indian Territory.

This campaign was doomed from the start. The Chickamauga warriors accomplished a victory over General Martin's forces, many of whom deserted or refused to fight under his leadership. The repulse of this sizable army was considered a great victory by Dragging Canoe and his brother Chiefs: John Watts, Bloody Fellow, Young Kitegisky, Glass, Little Owl, The Beaver, and Richard Justice. Martin's men were harassed all the way back to the settlements.

This victory encouraged the Indians to believe they could beat white men's armies, so bigger plans were made. A Cherokee army of 1,200, supported by a Creek Cavalry of 400 mounted warriors commanded by Tory officers, suddenly appeared on the horizon. Reports of this force advancing on the lower white settlements sent families fleeing to the safety of the nearest fort. A division of the red army under John Watts did capture Gillespie's Station; but attacks on Houston and White forts were beaten off. Hanging Maw, now serving as Principal Chief to the upper Indian settlements, appeared on the scene with a proclamation endorsed by North Carolina and Congress. Promising that the terms of the Hopewell Treaty would be enforced, the proclamation forbade "all unwarrantable intrusion and hostile proceedings against the Cherokee and ordered all whites settled on Cherokee land south of the French Broad River to leave or stay at their own peril." The Indian army was disbanded as such.

Dragging Canoe and his Chickamaugans didn't believe or trust the North Carolina and Congressional promises and continued with their own plans. The Cherokee Nation was still divided into two camps — peace and war. After Old Tassel's murder the Cherokee capital had been moved to Ustanali, located on the Coosawatie River near its junction with the Conasauga. Dragging Canoe's warriors continued their harassment of frontier settlers in Kentucky, the Cumberland, and lower regions of the State of Franklin territory.

The thousands of inhabitants who had settled in the lower areas of the Franklin territory had other ideas about the Government proclamation which ordered them off the rich fertile lands where they had staked their claims and built their cabins. They met at Newell's Station and organized the *Council of Safety*, electing John Sevier as their leader. Sevier was not present at the meeting as he was mustering a force on Buffalo Creek a hundred miles northeast of Newell's Station.

The Chickamaugans, encouraged by victories over Martin's force, success at Gillespie's Station, and other favorable events, decided on a bold move. They did not return to their town homes as was their usual winter custom. Instead, they established winter quarters on Flint Creek in Greasy Cove [Unicoi County, Tennessee]. This location in Rocky Fork gorge provided not only a secluded campsite, but convenient passes through which warrior bands could slip in and out when making raids on unsuspecting settlers.

Spies had reported this diversion to John Sevier, who mustered his men on Buffalo Creek near present Milligan College, Tennessee. When everything was ready, Colonel Sevier led his men approximately thirty miles through deep snow and extremely cold temperature to the location of the Indian encampment.

Sevier sent General McCarter with his *Bloody Rangers* up Devil's Fork Trail, to close off this upper pass through which the Indians could escape. The main body of troops closed off the lower entrance into the gorge. At a given signal the battle began, and the surprised Indians found their means of retreat cut off from both ends of the valley. They fought the whites desperately, returning such deadly fire that Sevier had to change his tactics. Troops mounted on horses were sent charging through the Indian lines and used swords and tomahawks with savage success. Many hand-to-hand fights took place all through the gorge.

Colonel Sevier later stated that the Flint Creek engagement was the bloodiest of all his thirty-five Indian battles during the Cherokee War. He reported that they buried 145 Indian warriors, while the Frontier army lost five killed and sixteen wounded.

SOUTHWEST TERRITORY

The North Carolina Legislature ratified the Constitution in 1789 and ceded their western territory (Tennessee) to Congress. This event opened the doors for diplomatic games of conquest for the control of the Mississippi Valley and all western lands. Leaders, who became active in western expansion, were to use methods that were varied, contradictory and unorthodox.

The Indians stated repeatedly, "We want nothing from the Amerians but justice. We want our hunting grounds preserved from encroachment; they have been ours from the beginning of time."

Secretary of War, General Knox, stated in a letter to President George Washington:
> The disgraceful violation of the "Treaty of Hopewell" with the Cherokee Indians requires the serious consideration of Congress. If so direct and manifest contempt for the authority of the United States be suffered with impunity, it will be in vain to attempt to extend the arm of the government to the frontiers. Indian tribes can have no faith in such imbecile promises, and lawless whites will ridicule a government which shall make Indian treaties and regulate Indian boundaries on paper only. [American State Papers, Indian Affairs]

The Indians of the Southeast were bewildered at the continued encroachment on their lands and the ruthless methods used by border militia groups in the destruction of their settlements, homes and crops. One chief described the aftermath of such a raid in this manner: "We are like wolves, ranging about in the woods to get something to eat. There is nothing to be seen in our towns but bones, weeds and grass."

James Seagrove, serving as Federal Agent to the Creek Nation in 1789, summed up existing situations among all southeast tribal societies in this report to President Washington:
> It is to be regretted that the insatiable rage of our frontier brethren for extending their limits cannot be checked and kept within the bounds set for them by the general government. The United States, like most countries, is unfortunate in having the worst of people on her frontiers, where there is the least energy to be expected in civil government, and where, unless supported by military force, civil authority becomes a nullity. [American State Papers, Indian Affairs, Vol. 1]

President Washington appointed William Blount as Governor of the territory south of the River Ohio (Southwest Territory) in June 1790. Blount was instructed to make peace with the Indians at almost any price. This order faced difficult solutions because frontiersmen, who made up the population of the Territory, were determined to get the Indian lands by any methods possible, legal or illegal. President Washington also asked the Senate for authority either to enforce the terms of the *Hopewell Treaty* or arrange new boundary lines that would include existing white settlements, pay the Cherokee for land that had been settled without official authority, and establish positive boundary lines for all time. Congress authorized this course of action in August 1790.

Governor Blount also served as Indian Agent during his term as Territorial Governor. In June of 1791 Blount arranged with James Robertson and Joseph Martin to meet with the Cherokee Council and invite all the Chiefs to attend a Treaty Meet at White's Fort [Knoxville, Tennessee] in early July 1791. Welcoming this move by the Federal Government, the Cherokee entertained high hopes that their day of justice had arrived and congressional promises would be fulfilled. Forty Chiefs attended, accompanied by more than 1,200 warriors, women, and children.

The occasion is said to have been an elaborate affair. Governor Blount, in full military dress, was seated under a canopy where he received each Chief individually. Trooper James Armstrong, serving as master of ceremonies, introduced each Chief by his full Indian name. By design, no soldiers were present; but a large number of white settlers attended. Chiefs John Watts and Bloody Fellow had been appointed as treaty speakers. From Brown's *Old Frontiers* we quote the following:

> John Watts spoke first, "I know that the North Carolina people are headstrong. Under the sanction of a flag of truce they laid low my Uncle, Old Tassel. It is vain for us to contend about a line. The North Carolina people will have their way, and will not observe orders of Congress or anyone else.... When you North Carolinians make a line, you tell us it is a standing one, but you are always encroaching on it and we cannot depend upon what you say."
>
> Governor Blount, somewhat angered, replied, "The lands were taken from the Cherokee in time of war, and I do not consider the settlements to be encroachments."

John Watts, greatly moved by the mention of the death of his uncle, Old Tassel, asked Bloody Fellow to continue to talk. Governor Blount repeated his statement: "You know, Bloody Fellow, the lands have been conquered, the Americans drove the English from this country, and the land has been purchased with American blood."

Bloody Fellow replied: "It is true that the English were driven from the country, but the French helped the Americans do it...."

Seven days passed before a treaty, already drawn up by Governor Blount, was signed. By its terms the country within the forks of Holston and French Broad Rivers, present site of Knoxville, and all lands north of the Little Tennessee River were ceded to the Americans. The Cherokee, still living in Chota, were separated from white settlements only by the width of the river. Surveyors with their compasses were busy laying off white land boundaries. Hanging Maw called the white man's compass "a land stealer."

Proceedings at the Treaty of Holston, from *American State Papers, Indian Affairs,* Vol. 1, list the Indian signers as: Scolacuta, Hanging Maw; Kunokeskie, John Watts; Nenetooyah, Bloody Fellow; Chuqualatague, Doublehead; Chuleoah, the Boots; Ocuma, the Badger; Enola, Black Fox; Nontuaka, Northward; Tekakiskee, Water Hunter; Tuckaseh, Terrapin; Kateh; Kunochatutloh, the Crane; Cauquelehanah, the Thigh; Chesqua-Telana, Yellow Bird; Chickasaw-tahee, Chickasaw Killer; Chutlow, Kingfisher; Toowa-yelloh, Bold Hunter; Tsale-oono-yeh-ka, Middlestriker; Kennesaw, the Cabin; Talli-tahee, Two Killer; Kealooske, Stopped Still; Kulsa-tahee, Creek Killer; Aquo-tague, Little Turkey's Son; Toonau-naloh; Testeekee, the Disturber; Robert McLemore; Skiuga, the Ground Squirrel; Tuckshalene; Tuskega-tahee, Tuskega Killer; Sawuteh, the Slave Catcher; Ancoowah, the Big Pigeon; Oosenaleh; Kenoteta, the Rising Fawn; Koolaqua, Big Acorn; Yona-watleh, Bear at Home; Long Will; Taloteeskee, the Upsetter; Chia-koneskie, Otter Lifter; Keshu-kaunee, She Rules.

The Cherokee were disappointed with the Holston Treaty, feeling that they had been tricked. They soon learned that Governor Blount, beneath his polite demeanor, was a frontier opportunist with little feeling for their human rights. Before long they were calling him the "Dirt Captain" and a greedy land grabber.

DRAGGING CANOE — STRONG MAN OF THE NATION

Chickamauga's growth and power, under Dragging Canoe's leadership, reached its peak during the years 1788-1790. The War Chief's fame as a staunch, courageous warrior and organizer was well established among eastern tribes, both north and south. Chiefs and warriors of the Creeks, Choctaws, and Shawnee respected Dragging Canoe as the strong man of the Cherokee-Chickamauga Nation. His name, as well as those of his Lieutenants — Bob Benge, John Watts, The Glass, Turtle at Home, Richard Justice, The Bench, Doublehead, Black Fox and others — cast fear throughout the white frontier. The Canoe depended on these Chiefs to carry on the fight against the Americans; and his two brothers, Little Owl and The Badger, served him faithfully as emissaries to neighboring tribes and friendly northern chiefs.

The Badger and his party of Chickamauga braves had returned home after participating in the defeat of General St. Clair on the banks of the Wabash in November 1791. His story of the battle related how a united force of tribal warriors under Chief Little Turtle's leadership defeated a white American army numbering 1,400 soldiers. This was just the spark Dragging Canoe needed to revive the war spirits of the southern Indians in their fight against the frontier Americans. With hopes of establishing a southern federation of tribal societies, the Canoe began visiting the chiefs of the neighboring tribes with talk of joining forces in their fight for survival. The Creeks and Choctaws gave pledges of cooperation, but the Chickasaws refused to take part.

When Dragging Canoe returned home late in February 1792, The Glass and Turtle at Home had just returned from raids in the Cumberland and Kentucky settlements, bringing white scalps. With war dances and scalp dances being staged in most of the principal Chickamauga towns, Dragging Canoe and his braves attended the celebration at Lookout Mountain Town. The frenzied, vigorous, excited dancing lasted all night, with the Eagle Tail Dance being performed as a special tribute to the War Chief.

The next day, March 1, 1792, Dragging Canoe was dead. It could have been the exertion of the all-night dancing or the result of wounds received during past battles, but the Cherokee-Chickamauga War Chief was gone. From the day of his declaration of a "dark and bloody settlement" during the Sycamore Shoals Treaty (1775), the Canoe never wavered from his avowed purpose of driving the Americans from Cherokee land. He had consistently refused to sign any treaty deeds or barter away the land of his people.

When told of Dragging Canoe's death, Governor Blount said: "Dragging Canoe stood second to none in his Nation." In an article titled, "Notable Persons in Cherokee History" in the *Journal of Cherokee Studies*, Volume 11, No. 1, E. Raymond Evans says:

> At the beginning of the American Revolution it had seemed that the Cherokee might be completely exterminated, or at best survive only as a beaten and degenerate people like the Catawba. This disaster was avoided by the firm holding action fought by Dragging Canoe. It was his determined resistance that made the Treaty of Tellico Blockhouse workable. Having felt the strength of the Cherokees, the whites respected the treaty for more than a generation. This period of peace made possible the brilliant flowering of Cherokee culture during the first quarter of the nineteenth century. . . . The Cherokee culture which Dragging Canoe and the Chickamauga Cherokee devoted their lives to saving is still very much alive. Today their descendants in Oklahoma and the mountains of North Carolina can still repeat with great pride Dragging Canoe's statement to the Shawnee delegation: "We are not yet conquered."

Some writers have suggested that the sixty-year-old Chief might have been given burial rites accorded to ranking Chiefs who died a natural death. James Adair, in his *History of the American Indian*, gives this summary of the burial ceremony of a Cherokee Chief:

> The body is washed and clothed in the Chief's best garments. The hair is anointed with bear's oil and the face painted red. The body is seated on animal skins outside his winter home, facing west. His most cherished possessions are placed around him. A prominent headsman, usually a kinsman, delivers a eulogy on the achievements and deeds of the dead leader. Then the body is borne three times around the place of interment, with the Medicine Man leading the procession. Relatives and friends follow behind. At each complete round, the Medicine Man pauses and commends the body to the Master of Life. When this part of the ceremony is finished the dead Chief is placed in his grave or tomb, in a seated position, facing east. His gun, bow, and quiver made of panther skin, filled with

arrows, pipe, tobacco, and other useful articles, along with food for the journey are placed in the grave. His widow visits the grave daily during the first month, to mourn his going.

At the time of Dragging Canoe's death, Chief John Watts was in Chota, talking with Governor Blount. Efforts were being made to win back the friendship of the Chickamauga towns; so Blount invited Watts and other Headmen of the Lower Towns to attend the proposed Coyatee meet in May 1792. Two messengers arrived in Chota during the conference, to inform Watts of Dragging Canoe's death and also tell him that the Chickamauga Council of Chiefs had chosen him as War Chief to succeed Dragging Canoe. The Council had requested his immediate return.

John Watts was all Indian despite his mixed blood. The red man's code, law, and practice were governing forces in his life. With a fair education for the times, Watts could speak both languages and was considered one of the great speechmakers of the Cherokee Nation. He knew the ways of the white man's diplomacy and double-dealing talks. The new War Chief would demonstrate leadership and organizational ability during the coming years, determined to continue the war plan of Dragging Canoe in the fight for Cherokee survival.

For more than two years John Watts continued the war against the Americans, then suddenly found that he had reached the end of the trail. Spanish authorities would not furnish his warriors with more supplies; his principal towns had been burned; and their northern allies were defeated by General Anthony Wayne. War Chief John Watts suddenly did an about face trying diplomatic efforts to reach a solution for a bad situation. Arrangements were made with Governor William Blount for a peace treaty meet at Tellico Block House November 7-8, 1794; and this treaty brought to a close the long, bitter, bloody warfare between the Cherokee and the Americans.

EXCERPTS FROM THE PAST

A few recorded glimpses of Nancy Ward during the 1790s are available from notes furnished by William Martin, son of Joseph Martin, and included in the Draper manuscripts from which excerpts are herewith inserted.

> When I, (William Martin) lived in South Carolina, (1791-1798) Bryant Ward, then old, sensible and intelligent, lived my neighbor — was settled, and had a family. He had, in early life, been a trader among the Cherokee. He took a wife there, the notorious Nancy Ward, spoken of before and the same referred to by Haywood. She was, as I think, one of the most superior women I ever saw. [Meaning apart from the advantages of Education, etc.]
>
> Bryant Ward and his family recognized her, for I have frequently seen her there; we then living not far from the Cherokee Settlements.

General Joseph Martin a native of Virginia was appointed first as Indian Agent from Virginia and later North Carolina. For a period he served as Indian Agent for both states. He married, partly for political reasons no doubt, (Elizabeth) a daughter of Nancy Ward.

Nancy Ward had a son by Kingfisher who was called 'Little Fellow' being small. Her brother was called 'Long Fellow' being tall. Both were distinguished warriors. I have seen them both. They were brother and uncle-in-law of my Father. After my Father was appointed Agent and married into the family they became acquainted and talked the matter over.

Nancy had a son by Kingfisher her first husband. The son was called 'Little Fellow' because during his youth he was very small. His Indian name was 'Hiskyteechee.' He was given the name 'Five Killer' when he became a Chief. Nancy Ward's brother, being tall was called 'Long Fellow.' His Indian name was 'Tuskeeteechee.' It is said that Long Fellow once ruled over seven towns and had influence over many other towns which listened to his talks.

It is said Long Fellow was living near Five Killer's place when Nancy Ward died. An old legend indicates that Nancy Ward's last days were spent in her brother Long Fellow's home near the Ocoee River.

When Bryant Ward separated from his wife Nancy he settled on Tugaloo River, South Carolina, where they were living in the 1790's. [Tugaloo River forms a boundary line between South Carolina and Georgia.] It is said that Nancy Ward visited the Bryant Ward family on several different occasions and was received with great respect by Ward's white family.

Annie Walker Burns includes in her Nancy Ward records a will signed by Bryant (his mark) Ward who died in 1808. The will is registered in Franklin County, Georgia. There are also records of land sales and grants signed by Bryant (his mark) Ward listed in the same record books. Annie Burns says this may or may not be the same Bryant Ward who married Nancy. These records were furnished by Edna Manley Phillips, Franklin County Historian. Madeline Kneberg lists Bryant Ward as a Georgia trader.

William Martin, son of General Joseph Martin, wrote of Cherokee affairs as follows:

In my other communications, I purposely omitted a pretty important item, in the history of my Father's life, from a wish to throw a veil over it; but on reflection, concluded to give the particulars: viz: When he (Joseph Martin) was appointed Agent to the Cherokee, he took a young half-breed Cherokee, by name of Betsy Ward, to wife. She was of the most distinguished clan of the whole tribe, and one of the finest families of that clan (for there was then, as marked distinction between families among them, as in civilized life.)

Her mother Nancy Ward was said to have more character than any woman there of her day — was wealthy, etc. With this woman (Betsy Ward) he lived the greater part of his long Agency... mostly at Long Island, [Kingsport, Tennessee] but sometimes in the Nation. Once in a while he would go home to Virginia, stay awhile and return. And strange as it may seem, it never produced any discord between him and my mother; such was her affection for him, and such was his address that he quited all concerned except myself...

By this Indian woman he had a son and daughter, very promising. When he left the Agency, he took the boy home to Virginia and raised and educated him, with the other children; and at my insistence he enlarged his education, to a knowledge of the classics; as he was promising, hoping, that, with these advantages he might, when grown be of advantage to his people. But, after getting his education, he went to the Nation, and disappointed all our hopes, and turned out badly. The girl married a respectable white man, and did well.

Chota, birthplace of Nancy Ward and Cherokee Town of Sanctuary, has been mentioned by most historians as becoming the Capital of the Cherokee Nation in 1730. David H. Corkran says in *The Cherokee Frontier: Conflict and Survival* as reprinted from *American Antiquity*, Vol. 37, No. 2, April, 1972:

Chota came into existence as a town between 1730 and 1740, although scattered homesteads may have been present in the area prior to that time. After a long power struggle with Great Tellico, Chota became the capital in 1753 through the superior diplomatic abilities of its council....

NANCY WARD'S PHILOSOPHY BEARS FRUIT

Tennessee became the sixteenth State in 1796, a fact which naturally changed the status of William Blount as Territorial Governor and Superintendent of Cherokee Indian Affairs. Benjamin Hawkins was appointed as *Principal Temporary Agent for Southern Indians* that same year. Hawkins made his headquarters at Colerain Military Post on St. Mary's River in Alabama. This post was located within the Creek Nation's territory; and a commission composed of Benjamin Hawkins, George Clymer and Andrew Pickens had concluded a Peace Treaty with that tribe on June 14, 1796.

Benjamin Hawkins was one of the four commissioners who conducted that first Federal-Cherokee Treaty at Hopewell, South Carolina, in 1785. Other commission members were Joseph Martin, Nancy Ward's son-in-law; Andrew Pickens; and Lachlan McIntosh. It can be safely assumed that Nancy Ward became acquainted with Benjamin Hawkins at the Hopewell Meet, where she made a notable talk before the commissioners.

For many years Nancy Ward had advocated the necessity for her people to devote more attention to farming and raising stock as a means of survival. Cherokee men were prejudiced against cows (the white man's buffalo) and also resented the necessary hard work of building fences to keep the cows out of their cornfields. Another objection was that cow meat could not be preserved by means of salt as easily as pork. Progress in this undertaking was very slow in the beginning, but Nancy Ward had planted the seeds of growth in fertile soil. Iron plows, hoes, seed, and qualified technicians were furnished the Cherokee Nation as promised by Article Fourteen of the Holston Treaty:

> Article 14. That the Cherokee nation may be led to a greater degree of civilization, and to become herdsmen and cultivators, instead of remaining in a state of hunters, the United States will, from time to time, furnish gratuitously the said nation with useful implements of husbandry. And further, to assist the said nation in so desirable a pursuit, and at the same time to establish a certain mode of communication, the United States will send such, and so many, persons to reside in said nation, as they may judge proper, and not exceeding four in number, who shall qualify themselves to act as interpreters. These persons shall have lands assigned them by the Cherokees for cultivation, for themselves and their successors in office; but they shall be precluded exercising any kind of traffic.

William Bartram, noted naturalist-explorer, wrote in 1789: "If adopting or imitating the manners and customs of the white man is to be termed civilization, perhaps the Cherokee have made the greatest advance." Theodore Roosevelt later said, "The Cherokee are a bright intelligent race, better fitted to 'follow the white man's road' than any other Indians."

Benjamin Hawkins made his first tour through the Cherokee Nation in November 1796. He found the natives receptive to new ideas of improvement. Before President George Washington left office, he expressed hopes and made plans that would help the Cherokee become more self-sustaining. Washington's successor, John Adams, attempted to follow the guidelines planned by President Washington. Soon, artisans went to the Nation to make spinning wheels and looms for the women, and after making the implements taught the women how to use them.

During the year 1799, Steiner and Schweinitz, two Moravian missionaries, visited the Cherokee Nation and made this report in their journal as recorded by Judge Williams in *Early Travels in Tennessee*:

> Before we reached Wachowee (Chestowee) we crossed a broad, clear stream, which is a branch of the Hiwassee. Passing by several houses, we dismounted at the home of Mrs. Martin (The Indian wife of General Joseph Martin and daughter of Bryant and Nancy Ward.) but heard, at the same time, to our regret, that she was gone on a visit to her father, five days journey distant. She has her home on a fine plantation along the river. Here are four houses close together, with a well kept yard between. Before reaching the houses, we had to pass through a lane with high fences and shut off by two drop-gates. Her cousin, by the name of Walker, who speaks English well, received us kindly.
>
> The house of Mrs. Martin is built up of hewn logs, well chinked and covered inside with white clay. The fireplace is of stone. The furnishings consisted of two bedsteads with bedding, woven chairs, a table of walnut-wood and a closet with tin and china ware. All appeared clean and in order. We saw there also cotton carding combs and spun cotton. . . . The fields lie mostly on high level ground and are well

fenced in. The corn fields were plowed and cleared of grass; the wheat had been sown, and we saw a field of turnips. The inhabitants of this region have horses, cattle, hogs, fowl, dogs and cats. Our hosts had also negro slaves that were well clothed, bright, lively and appeared to be happy and well cared for. These conducted themselves toward us and toward the Indians, with all courtesy. Cotton is raised and spun here. In one house there was a loom for weaving.

Another innovation that had been promised the Cherokee was brought to the Hiwassee area during the late 1790s in the form of a water-powered grain mill. Federal agents employed a German named John Hildebrand to erect a grain mill at government expense, and Hildebrand was to show the Indians how to raise and process wheat for bread.

Another excerpt from the journal of the Moravian Missionaries states:

A man named Friderici served as our guide at Hiwassee and nearby area. He accompanied us about a quarter of a mile from town to a rocky creek with considerable fall to the place where Mr. Hildebrand intends to build the mill and whose house is on an elevation about three quarters of a mile from here. He (Mr. Hildebrand) is not at home, having gone to Knoxville, Tennessee, in order to have mill-irons made, which with the mill-stones are to be brought here by water.

John Hildebrand, of Dutch-German descent, had moved here from western North Carolina after the death of his Dutch wife. His five children were Michael, Peter, John, George, and Sarah. He later married an Indian woman named Susan Householder. Two of John Hildebrand's German sons married granddaughters of Nancy Ward. Michael married Nannie Martin, and Peter married Elizabeth (Betsy) Harlan. [Penelope Allen, State Historian for Tennessee D.A.R. for many years, produced an outstanding genealogy of Hildebrand descendants.]

Several attempts were made during the last half of the eighteenth century to establish mission schools and churches within the Cherokee Nation. None were successful. Because of war and other obstacles it was the early years of the nineteenth century before much was accomplished. The Moravians started the first school at Spring Place, Georgia, in 1801, and another at a later date at Oothcaloga, Georgia, near the present town of Calhoun. The American Board of Commissioners for Foreign Missions (Interdenominational) founded a mission school at Brainerd, Tennessee. (The site is now known as Missionary Ridge in Chattanooga, Tennessee.) The Presbyterian Church appointed Gideon Blackburn as Missionary to the Cherokee. With offerings and help from the Presbyterian General Assembly, Blackburn operated two schools — one at Hiwassee Garrison and the other at Sale Creek. The Baptists founded a school in the Valley Towns, western North Carolina at Old Natchez, and another on Coosawatee River near its mouth in Georgia.

During the first quarter of the nineteenth century another event occurred that placed the Cherokee Nation out front among American Indian Tribes — the invention of the Cherokee Syllabary by Sequoyah. The inventer spent twelve years completing his eighty-five symbol syllabary (often referred to as Cherokee alphabet). Sequoyah submitted it to public test before leading men of the Nation in 1821, about a year before the death of Nancy Ward. Six years after Nancy's death the first issue of the *Cherokee Phoenix* (Cherokee newspaper) was published at new Echota. In his historical notes, page 219, item 40, Mooney wrote concerning Sequoyah's Cherokee Syllabary:

In the various schemes of symbolic thought representation, from the simple pictograph of the primitive man to the finished alphabet of the civilized nations, our own system, although not yet perfect, stands at the head of the list, the result of three thousand years of development by Egyptian, Phoenician, and Greek. Sequoya's syllabary, the unaided work of an uneducated Indian reared amid semisavage surroundings, stands second.

Twelve years of his life are said to have been given to his great work. Being entirely without instruction and having no knowledge of the philosophy of language, being not even acquainted with English, his first attempts were naturally enough in the direction of the crude Indian pictograph. He set out to devise a symbol for each word of the language, and after several years of experiment, finding this an utterly hopeless task, he threw aside the thousands of characters which he had, carved or scratched upon pieces of bark, and started in anew to study the construction of the language itself. By attentive observation for another long period he finally discovered that the sounds in the words used by the Cherokee in their daily conversation and their public speeches could be analyzed and classified, and that the thousands of possible words were all formed from varying combinations of hardly more than a hundred distinct syllables. Having thoroughly tested his discovery until satisfied of its correctness, he next proceeded to formulate a symbol for each syllable. For this purpose he made use of a number of characters which he found in an old English spelling book, picking out capitals, lower-case, italics, and figures, and placing them right side up or upside down, without any idea of their sound or significance as used in English. Having thus utilized some thirty-five ready-made characters, to which must be added a dozen or more produced by modification of the same originals, he designed from his own imagination as many more as were necessary to his purpose, making eighty-five in all.

NANCY WARD'S LAST COUNCIL MESSAGE

Nearly all Cherokee land treaty cessions occurred during Nancy Ward's lifetime. Two exceptions were (1) the 1721 cession to Governor Nicholson of South Carolina, and (2) the final cession of 1835, which occurred after her death. Nancy's lifespan covered a dramatic period in Cherokee history, during which their National Society was toppled from its position as the strongest Tribe among southeastern Indian Societies to a small Nation of disturbed, embittered, and divided people. Her last official message to the Council of Chiefs (included in this chapter) begged the Chiefs and all Cherokee people to keep their "hands off [white man's] paper talks," and discouraged any thought of moving to the west.

Immigrations westward by small Cherokee bands are thought to have started soon after the Revolutionary War and continued until the final removal in 1838. Legend says that one band of warriors and their families followed Chief Yunwi-Usago-Se-Ti (Dangerous Man) across the Mississippi River shortly after that first land cession in 1721. Dangerous Man evidently sensed, even then, the inevitable yielding to white domination.

Tribal unrest within the Nation had increased during the three decades following Dragging Canoe's death; and there was deep resentment between the progressives and the conservatives. The progressives were the farming families who were adapting to the civilizing policies of the Federal Government. The conservatives, or old liners, were still clinging to the old ways. The feelings became so intense that progressive leaders requested the Federal Government to establish a boundary line between the two differing groups, allowing the progressives to divide their lands into severalty and become citizens of the United States. Government officials, who were watching this situation closely, were kept informed by Indian Agents posted in the Nation.

Thomas Jefferson was sworn into office as President of the United States in 1801. Henry Dearborn, his Secretary of War, appointed General Return Jonathan Meigs as Cherokee Indian Agent in May of that same year, and he also accepted the office of Agent of the Federal War Department in Tennessee, positions he held until his death in 1823. Meigs' major responsibilites were to serve as a liaison officer between the two peoples, arrange treaty conferences for territorial cessions, direct civilizing programs for the Indians, and serve as an elder brother to the Cherokee.

In 1803 President Jefferson consummated the Louisiana Purchase from the French, which included land between the Mississippi River and the Rocky Mountains, from the Canadian border to the Gulf of Mexico. Because of increasing pressure from the states bordering the Cherokee Nation, President Jefferson suggested to Congress the possiblity and desirability of moving all Indian Tribes east of the Mississippi River to the newly acquired lands west of the river.

The states of Tennessee, Georgia, and the Carolinas, as well as many members of Congress, were more than just interested in removal plans. They wanted to be rid of the Indians as soon as possible. In 1797 the State of Tennessee addressed a memorial to Congress asking, "that Indian titles in that State be extinguished at the earliest possible moment, that the Indians at best were but tenants at will, and that treaties guaranteeing them their lands were contrary to the rights of Tennessee," [*American State Papers, Indian Affairs*, Vol. I, p. 625]. Warrant holders in both North Carolina and Tennessee wanted the Indians removed in order to claim their land.

Georgia ceded her western territory to the Federal Government in 1802, and almost immediately State officials began pressuring Federal authorities to expel the Cherokee. For thirty years following the 1802 cession to Congress, Georgians, with increasing impatience, insisted that the Federal Government move both the Cherokee and the Creeks off the ceded land and honor the *Compact of 1802*.

Working with Federal appointed commissioners during the years 1804-1807, Meigs helped arrange several Cherokee cessions which included: a small tract in Georgia called the Wafford Settlement, lands in Kentucky and Middle Tennessee, a tract between the Tennessee and Duck Rivers, and the Long Island on the Holston River (Kingsport, Tennessee). These cessions contained over 8,000 square miles of Indian territory. Bribery and silent considerations induced some prominent Cherokee Chiefs to sign the cession papers; these were not official cessions by the Cherokee Council. On one occasion $1,000 and several rifles were given to unofficial signers, who had been mellowed with rum before the transaction.

Doublehead, a leading culprit in the 1805-1806 deals, was assassinated by Council orders within a year or so. Other signers fled west for safety. Members of the Cherokee Council went to Washington and protested these treaties as illegal, but Congress ratified them in spite of the objections.

During the summer of 1808 General Meigs was in Washington with a Cherokee delegation. The Secretary of War instructed him to use his persuasive influence to get the Cherokee to trade their eastern lands for western land. Though he did not have much success with the land exchange plan, Meigs did persuade many families to move west. They had to do this at their own expense because Congress had appropriated no money for this purpose; but it is estimated that nearly 2,000 Cherokee had moved west by 1817.

During the terrible battle of Horseshoe Bend in March 1814, several hundred Cherokee were assisting the American Army against the Creeks. It was more a massacre than a battle. The Cherokee have claimed through the years that they saved General Andrew Jackson's army from defeat during this engagement. A participant in this battle was Chief Junaluska, a revered Chief of the Cherokee, especially among the Quala Boundary Indians of western North Carolina. Years later he said: "If I had known that Andrew Jackson would later drive us from our home I would have killed him that day at Horseshoe Bend."

Cherokee families who had already moved west were running into complications. The Osage Indian Tribe claimed the land north of the Arkansas River, and the Quapaws the land to the south; and both tribes resented the intrusion of the emigrating Cherokee. Hostile conflicts soon erupted, and western Cherokee complained to Congress about the situation. This problem gave General Andrew Jackson the necessary leverage to revive Indian removal interest and cession proposals in Congress. Jackson convinced Secretary of War Calhoun that the majority of the Cherokee people wanted to exchange their eastern land for western territory and move — a false ruse which succeeded. General Andrew Jackson, Governor Joseph McMinn, and General David Merewether were appointed as commissioners to handle the Cherokee treaties.

Cherokee-United States treaties (starting with the Hopewell Treaty of 1785 and all those that followed) were breached many times, both in letter and spirit, by the United States. Nothing the Indians might have done or left undone could have changed the course of events. Land boundaries, guaranteed by the Federal Government to the Indians, had to be surrendered time after time. Frontiersmen and many officials of those states bordering the Cherokee Nation even resented the establishment of schools and churches in the Nation. They felt that education and enlightenment would stiffen Indian resistance to their demands.

The land cessions of 1817-1819 were complicated affairs. With the official Cherokee Council stubbornly resisting more cessions to either the Untied States or bordering state authorities, the appointed commissioners resorted to bribery and illegal methods to get signers for the 1817 cessions. The 2,000 emigrants who had already moved west were told they could have no western land until an equivalent acreage had been ceded in the east. Because of this, fifteen western Cherokee Chiefs were persuaded to sign by proxy; while well-placed bribes and off-the-record promises enticed thirty-one eastern Chiefs to sign. These papers, signed at the Indian Agency (Calhoun, Tennessee) July 8, 1817, were used by the commissioners to secure several tracts in Tennessee, Georgia, and the Muscle Shoals area. The eastern Chiefs who signed the cession papers soon moved west, fearful for their lives.

This transaction was bitterly resented by the Cherokee Council, which met the first week in May 1817 at Cleveland, Tennessee. John Ross, well educated in both languages, was instructed to write a memorial to the commissioners expressing the Council's feelings and strongly protesting the proposed cessions. A new member of the Council, Ross was to become a strong leader during the reorganization of the Cherokee Government. It was at the May 6 council meet that the Tribal-Clan form of rule was discarded for the executive, legislative, and judicial process similar to that of the United States. In an 1820 session the Nation was divided into eight districts, which were laid off along geographical lines rather than population proportions. Ross was elected President of the upper house in 1820; and in 1828 he was elected titular head or Principal Chief of the Cherokee Nation, a position he held until his death.

John Ross prepared the memorial at the May 1817 session; and it was signed by sixty-seven Chiefs in official council action. The document was presented to the commissioners before the illegal signing of papers on July 8, 1817; but the commissioners paid no attention to the documents and completely disregarded the official Cherokee Council action. It seems rather obvious that his memorial was not included in the papers submitted to Congress.

The following document (not the council memorial) was sent by Nancy Ward to the Amovey Council session. It was later found in the Jackson Papers Book 29, No. 17, Vol 14, pg. 6452-3.

Amovey in council 2nd May 1817

A True Copy)

The Cherokee ladys now being present at the meeting of the Chiefs and warriors in council have thought it their duty as mothers to address their beloved chiefs and warriors now assembled.

Our beloved children and head men of the Cherokee nation we address you warriors in council we have raised all of you on the land which we now have, which God gave us to inhabit and raise provisions we know that our country has once been extensive but by repeated sales has become circumscribed to a small tract and never have thought it our duty to interfere in the disposition of it till now, if a father or mother was to sell all their lands which they had to depend on which their children had to raise their living on which would be indeed bad and to be removed to another country we do not wish to go to an unknown country which we have understood some of our children wish to go over the Mississippi but this act of our children would be like destroying your mothers. Your mothers your sisters ask and beg of you not to part with any more of our lands, we say ours you are descendants and take pity on our request, but keep it for our growing children for it was the good will of our creator to place us here and you know our father the great president will not allow his white children to take our country away only keep your hands off of paper talks for it is our own country for if it was not they would not ask you to put your hands to paper for it would be impossible to remove us all for as soon as one child is raised we have others in our arms for such is our situation and will consider our circumstance.

Therefore children don't part with any more of our lands but continue on it and enlarge your farms and cultivate and raise corn and cotton and we your mothers and sisters will make clothing for you which our father the president has recommended to us all we don't charge anybody for selling any lands, but we have heard such intentions of our children but your talks become true at last and it was our desire to forewarn you all not to part with our lands.

Nancy Ward to her children Warriors to take pity and listen to the talks of your sisters, although I am very old yet cannot but pity the situation in which you will hear of their minds, I have great many grand children which I wish them to do well on our land.

Attested
A McCoy Clk   )
)   Nancy Ward
Thos. Wilson Secty)
    Jenny McIntosh   Widow Tarpin
    Caty Harlan   Ally Critington
    Elizabeth Walker   Cun, o, ah
    Susanna Fox   Miss Asty Walker
    Widow Gunrod   Mrs. M. Morgan
    Widow Woman Holder Mrs. Nancy Fields

This was Nancy Ward's last message to the Cherokee Council and her final act as the Nation's Chief *Honored Woman*. Because of old age and illness it is said that Nancy's son, Five Killer, delivered her written message to the Council along with her 'distinctive walking cane' which represented her official vote when absent.

Delegation after delegation, representing the official Council, protested to Congress; but the illegally signed cessions were ratified anyway. Government officials did not let up; they were determined that the Cherokee be moved off their native land — lock, stock, and barrel. Governor McMinn was appointed to arrange transportation for those who promised to move west; and boats and provisions were assembled at key points for this purpose.

Governor McMinn also arranged a call session of the Cherokee Council in November 1818. Telling the assembled Chiefs that it was no longer possible to protect the Indians from the continuous harassment and encroachment of white people onto their lands, he said: "Your cattle will be stolen; women corrupted and the men made drunkards. Your only solution is to move to the western paradise." When he offered the Cherokee $100,000 for the whole of their remaining territory, the Council voted a unanimous "no." McMinn then doubled the offered amount, but the Council only gave him another indignant and more emphatic "no" vote. Even the women presented a strong petition (similar to Nancy Ward's) against selling and moving.

During the fall session of 1820 the Cherokee Council voted, by special decree, to abolish the right of blood revenge by clan ties; and it was made an act of treason, punishable by death, for any individual to negotiate the sale of Cherokee lands to whites without consent of the national council.

One stipulation of the 1817-1819 treaties was the reservation clause:

> Each head of a Cherokee family residing on lands herein or hereafter ceded to the United States who elects to become a citizen of the United States shall receive a reservation of six hundred and forty (640) acres to include his or her improvements for life, with reversion in fee simple to children, subject to widow's dower.

A large number of Cherokee accepted this provision and made request to the proper authorities. Nancy Ward was a recipient of such a reservation grant. Annie Walker Burns, compiler of *Military and Genealogical Records of the 'Famous Woman of Tennessee,' Nancy Ward* makes available the following document from the United States Archives Record Group number 75:

To Whom It May Concern;

> Nancy Ward a native of the Cherokee Nation did on the 19th day of November 1818 register her name in the Cherokee Agent's Office for the section of land one mile below John McIntosh's on Mouse Creek where the Old Trace crosses said creek leading from Tellico Block House to Hiwassee Garrison. Beginning at the ford and running down said creek for a compliment conformably to a treaty between the United States and the Cherokee Nation concluded on the 8th day of July 1817. Considering herself under the protection and amendable to the laws of the said United States which reservation is by her for divers causes and considerations bequeathed to her beloved Granddaughter Jenny McIntosh and her heirs forever.

> Given under my hand and seal of the Cherokee Agency this December 28th, 1818. Signed by H. or S. G. Williams, Bus. Agent--. On the back of the above paper: no 767.

> Nancy Ward's Heirs, Vs. Reservation No 156 the United States filed December 31. 1846.

> Decree (verdict) rendered May 27th, 1847. <u>Claim rejected.</u>

>   Signed W. S. Miller, Secretary

At bottom of page was written J. H. Eaton, Attorney.

Several hundred similar reservation grants were issued to those Indian families who presented requests to the proper authorities. Among the hundreds of names, besides Nancy Ward's, were Colonel George Lowery, Chief John Ross, Walter Adair, John Martin and John Hildebrand. The State of Tennessee flatly refused to recognize these individual reservation grants, however; while North Carolina and Georgia officials, with money furnished by Congress, simply bought up most of these reservations located in their states.

Many family heads, and descendants of those then dead, entered court suits in efforts to regain the reservation land. Lawyer Jarnigan presented a bill of $4,000.00 to the Government for legal services rendered the Cherokee Nation (1821-1837) in attending five or six hundred such cases in court arising from reservation grants under the treaty of 1817. [See Allen in Bibliography.]

One of the problems arising from reservation grants was the fact that white frontiersmen moved in on individual Indian family grants and, with harassment and persecution, forced the Indian families to leave their property and homes. Colonel George Lowery was forced to give up his home and Battle Creek plantation. John Hildebrand, who received his grant by marriage to a Cherokee woman, was forced to leave his reservation and move south of the Hiwassee River. Hildebrand registered a claim for improvements on the property, as promised by the Government, but was never able to collect. Near the bottom of Nancy Ward's grant is the following notation: "Nancy Ward's Heirs, Vs. Reservation No. 156 the United States, filed December 31, 1846. Decree (verdict) rendered May 27th, 1847. Claim rejected."

NANCY WARD'S LAST HOME

Very little information is available as to the actual date Nancy Ward moved from Chota to the Ocoee River location. A journal entry by Steiner and Schweinitz during their 1799 visit gives this description of Chota: "We came to Chota, where we could discover only five houses, which were scattered over the plain. Besides some women and children, we met only one old man, in front of his house, Arcowee by name, who is the beloved man of Chota." Two or three observations might help clarify this description of Chota relative to other developments of the 1790 decade. It was stated at the time of the Holston Treaty in 1791 that white settlements were already established on land across the Little Tennessee River from Chota; Cherokee towns and villages along the little Tennessee, Tellico, and Hiwassee Rivers had become more like farmstead settlements rather than compact groups of town houses; and most of the important or virile families had already moved farther south to get away from the increasing pressure of white encroachment and constant attacks of frontier militia.

The two Moravian missionaries also gave this description of the area as they traveled from Chota to the Tellico Blockhouse: "At all the houses we pased we saw fine cornfields, partly enclosed by low fences. The corn was mostly in cornsheds, built upon stakes. We also saw beans, pumpkins, white cabbage and some tobacco. The fields as well as the uncultivated land were overgrown with Rampion."

In *Haywood's Natural and Aboriginal History of Tennessee* reprinted in 1959 by Mary U. Rothrock, Editor, with end papers by Madeline Kneberg, Professor of Anthropology, University of Tennessee, Kneberg says in her annotations, chapter 10, page 423:

> Caleb Starr, who married Nancy Harlan, granddaughter of Nancy Ward, was born about 1758 in Chester County, Pennsylvania, and came to Tennessee about 1775 with Joseph McMinn, with whom he was closely associated. Starr lived on Conasauga Creek in present McMinn County, Tennessee. Nancy Ward (1737-1824) was a full-blood of the Wolf Clan, who by common consent became the *Beloved Woman* or *Ghigau* She first married Kingfisher; and after his death Bryan (Bryant) Ward, a Georgia trader. The basis for the tradition that she was the niece of Attakullakulla is unknown. In later life Nancy Ward operated an inn at her home, the Womankiller Ford on the Ocoee River near (present) Benton, Tennessee and became wealthy. She died there in the spring of 1824.

John Walker Hildebrand, great grandson of Nancy Ward and son of Peter and Elizabeth (Harlan) Hildebrand, was born February 23, 1818, in that part of the Cherokee Nation now Polk County, Tennessee (at the Cherokee village of *Uwaga-hi*, commonly called Ocoee) and died September 17, 1910, in Polk County, Tennessee. He was known as 'Uncle Jack' among a large circle of friends and neighbors. It is from his interesting *Recollections* about events during the nineteenth century that much of the local history of Polk County has been preserved. As a child of four years he attended the funeral of his great grandmother, Nancy Ward, the famous Cherokee Chieftainess, whose romantic life has become an important part of the history of her tribe. It was 'Uncle Jack' who located her grave in Polk County, which was marked in October 1923 by the Nancy Ward Chapter of the Daughters of the American Revolution.

Hildebrand's *Recollections* appeared in the *Chattanooga Times*, Chattanooga, Tennessee, in August or September 1924. They were published, as told to Jack Williams and M. O. Cates by 'Uncle Jack,' in 1908. Hildebrand says Nancy died in 1822.

Legend and most writers, like Madeline Kneberg, indicate that Nancy operated an inn at her home, the Womankiller Ford on the Ocoee River, and became wealthy. In connection with this legend several items are worth consideration: first, she had very little time to establish or operate an inn and become wealthy if she moved to the Ocoee area after the Hiwassee cession (which included the Chota site) in 1819; second, her last message to the Cherokee Council, dated May 2, 1817, is said to have been carried to the Council meeting by her son, Five Killer (legend indicates that because of Nancy Ward's age and ill health she could not attend); and third, roads for mail and other types of passage through the Nation were being opened during the first quarter of the nineteenth century, making travel easier. Therefore, to establish and operate an inn with much success, Nancy and her retinue must have moved into the Amovey District earlier than some writers have suggested.

It seems reasonable to assume that one of the prevailing reasons Nancy moved to the Amovey District of the Cherokee Nation was because so many of her family were already living in the Ocoee-Hiwassee area. For instance, two of John Hildebrand's sons by his Dutch wife married granddaughters of Nancy Ward. Michael married Nannie Martin and they became the parents of twelve children: Elizabeth, John, Jennie, Margaret, Delilah, Stephen, Rachel, Nannie, Joseph, Brice, Mary, and Michael. The other son, Peter, married Elizabeth Harlan and they became the parents of ten children: Barbara, James, Jennie, Catherine, John Walker (Uncle Jack), Ellis Harlan, Lewis W., Isaac, Mary Elizabeth, and Minerva. Also, the first three names signed to the document Nancy sent to the Council, dated May 2, 1817, were members of her family. Nancy's brother, Long Fellow, was a long time resident of the area according to A. V. Goodpasture. Her son Five Killer's cabin is also mentioned.

During her last years, Nancy was affectionately called 'Granny Ward' by her many descendants and neighbors. She continued to be, in the minds and hearts of those around her, Cherokee's *Most Honored Woman*.

Death and Burial

If Nancy Ward's obituary had been printed at the time of her death, it might have read someting like this:

> Nanye-hi was born to Tame Doe, sister of Attakullakulla in 1738 at Chota, long time Capital of the Cherokee Nation. She died in the Amovey District near the Ocoee River in 1822 at the home of her brother, Long Fellow, with whom (legend says) she was living at the time of her death. Nanye-hi (Anglicized to Nancy) first married Kingfisher; and they were the parents of Catherine and Five Killer. She next married Bryant Ward, a white trader. Nancy and Bryant had one daughter, Elizabeth Ward, who became the Indian wife of Colonel Joseph Martin. There were grandchildren and great grandchildren too numerous to mention. Interment of her body was in a grave located on land later called the M. H. Hancock farm, only a short distance from the historic *Old Indian War Trail*.

The story of Nancy Ward's death and funeral is told by her great grandson, 'Uncle Jack' Hildebrand. Born in February 1818, 'Uncle Jack' was four years old when Nancy died. In his *Recollections* and a sworn statement he tells of being in the room when "a light rose from her body, fluttered around the room like a bird, left through an open door and disappeared toward Chota. This was watched by those in attendance who were startled at this apparition."

From *Clemmer's Columns* (J. D. Clemmer, Benton, Tennessee) comes this description of the funeral. Most likely this information came from 'Uncle Jack.'

> The parents of Jack Hildebrand took the four-year-old boy to his Great-grandmother's funeral; he walked with his father, Peter Hildebrand along the 'old war path' from their home (now the McClary farm) across Four Mile Creek along the top of Wilson Hill, past Five Killer's cabin, crossing the Ocoee at 'Womankiller Ford' then along the war path up a little valley just northwest of Hancock Hill and turned aside to the left up the hill to an open grave soon to receive the remains of Nancy Ward. Uncle Jack remembered and wondered about the number of pots and pans placed in the grave to be used in the next world.

Nancy Ward's brother Long Fellow and her son Five Killer are buried in the same plot near her. Except for a few stones laid around, the graves were unmarked for approximately one hundred years; and it was 'Uncle Jack' who later located the three graves for preservation.

In Chattanooga, Tennessee, during 1915, a very active chapter of the Daughters of the American Revolution honored the famous Cherokee Chieftainess by naming their society the "Nancy Ward Chapter." In the fall of 1923 this DAR Chapter placed over her grave a pyramid of quartz field stones, in which a bronze tablet was embedded. A photograph showing the inscription is shown on the following page.

Remove not the ancient landmarks, which thy fathers have set. — Proverbs 22:28

Nancy Ward's grave is located in Polk County near Benton, Tennessee; Five Killer is buried nearby. Photos courtesy Harry D. Switzer.

BIBLIOGRAPHY

Adair, James: *History of the American Indian.* First published in London, England, 1775. Edited and published under auspice of National Society of Colonial Dames of America by Samuel Cole Williams, 1930. Reprinted by Blue and Gray Press, Nashville, Tennessee, 1971.

Alderman, Pat: *The Overmountain Men.* A capsule history of early Tennessee 1760-1796. Published by the Overmountain Press, Box 1261, Johnson City, Tennessee, 1970.

Allen, Penelope J.: *Leaves from the Family Tree.* The Allen papers include genealogies of the *Lowery Family — Vann Family — Hildebrand Family.* A collection of materials on Cherokee History such as *Claim Papers* and *The Record Book of the Cherokee Nations*

Supreme Court 1823-1835. Papers concerning petition of Attorney Jarnigan for legal services rendered Cherokee Nation for $4,000. This service was for representing four or five hundred cases arising from Cherokee Reservations under treaties of 1817-1819. The Chattanooga Times carried much of this material in the magazine section during the 1930s. Copies of the family trees mentioned are said to be available in Knoxville, Tennessee, and Chattanooga, Tennessee, Libraries; also Tennessee State Library, Nashville, Tennessee.

American State Papers: Class 11, Indian Affairs (2 volumes) Documents Legislative and Executive, of the Congress of the United States, December 4, 1815-March 3, 1827, Washington, D.C.

Brown, John P.: *Old Frontiers*. The story of the Cherokee Indians from earliest times to the date of their removal to the West in 1838. Southern Publishers, Inc., Kingsport, Tennessee, 1938.

Burns, Annie Walker: *Military and Genealogical Records of the Famous Woman of Tennessee, Nancy Ward*. This is a mimeographed collection of items related to Nancy Ward and the Cherokee Nation, Washington, D.C., 1957.

Carter, Clarence E., Editor: *The Territory South of the River Ohio, 1790-1796 Volume IV, The Territorial Papers of the United States*. Washington: United States Printing Office, 1930.

Clemer, J.D.: Scrapbook and various newspaper columns concerning local history of Polk County, last home and burial place of Nancy Ward. Microfilm Tennessee State Library, Nashville, Tennessee. Cleveland Community College, Cleveland, Tennessee.

Collier, Thompson: *Indians of the Americas* W.W. Norton and Co. Inc. and New American Library of the World Literature, A Mentor Book, fifth printing 1956.

Draper, Lyman C.: Various papers and manuscripts, Wisconsin Historical Society. Tennessee Documents can be found at Lawson McGee Library, Knoxville, Tennessee.

Driver, Harold E.: *Indians of North America*. The University of Chicago Press, Chicago, Illinois, 1961-1969.

Evans, E. Raymond: "Dragging Canoe," *Notable Persons in Cherokee History*. Journal of Cherokee Studies, Vol. 11, No. 1, Winter 1977. Published by Museum of the Cherokee Indian in cooperation with the Cherokee Historical Association, Cherokee, North Carolina.

Fink, Paul M.: Various publications and manuscripts in Tennessee Historical Quarterly, Nashville, Tennessee.

Foreman, Carolyn Thomas: *Indian Women Chiefs*. Chapter 7 is devoted to Nancy Ward, Beloved Woman of the Cherokee Nation for more than half a century. Printed by Star Printery, Inc., Muskogee, Oklahoma, 1954.

Foreman, Grant: *Indian Removal* also a collection of Pioneer and Indian papers of recorded interviews of approximately 2500 aged Cherokee. This was a WPA project supervised by Foreman. Library of University of Oklahoma.

Goodpasture, A.V.: "Indian Wars and Warriors," *Tennessee Historical Magazine*, Volume 4, Nashville, Tennessee.

Hawkins, Benjamin, Letters of: Volume 4, Collections of the Georgia Historical Society, Savannah, Georgia.

Haywood, John: *The Civil and Political History of Tennessee from the Earliest Settlement up to the Year 1796*. Knoxville, Tennessee (reprints).

Natural and Aboriginal History of Tennessee. Reprinted by Mary U. Rothrock, Editor. End papers drawn by Madeline Kneberg, Professor of Anthropology, University of Tennessee, Knoxville, Tennessee. Reprint by McCowat-Mercer Press, Inc., Jackson, Tennessee, 1959.

Kappler, Charles J.: *Indian Treaties*, Volume 11, Indian Affairs: Laws and Treaties, Senate Document No. 319, Washington, D.C., United States Printing Office, 1904.

Kneberg, Madeline and Thomas M.N. Lewis: *Tribes That Slumber*. Published by University of Tennessee Press, Knoxville, Tennessee 1958 (reprints 1960-1966).

Lillard, Roy G.: "The Story of Nancy Ward," *Daughters of the American Revolution Magazine*, January, 1976.

Lindneux, Robert: *Trail of Tears*. Courtesy Woolaroc Museum, Bartlesville, Oklahoma.

Malone, Henry Thompson: *Cherokee of the Old South.* A people in transition, The University of Georgia Press, Athens, Georgia, 1956.

McClary, Ben Harris: *Nancy Ward: The Last Beloved Woman of the Cherokee.* Tennessee Historical Quarterly #21, 1962.

Mooney, James: *Myths of the Cherokee*, Nineteenth Annual Report of the Bureau of American Ethnology, 1897-98 (Washington: Government Printing Office, 1900) Part I, 11-586, is based upon much research and also the experience of living among the Cherokee of the Qualla Boundary in North Carolina. A very valuable source of reference. Reprint 1972 by Charles Eller — Bookseller — Publisher, Nashville, Tennessee.

Nammack, Georgianna C.: *Frauds, Politics and Dispossessions of the Indians*, published by University of Oklahoma Press, Norman, Oklahoma, 1969.

Ramsey, J.G.M.: *The Annals of Tennessee* to the end of the 18th Century. Charleston, South Carolina (reprints).

Roosevelt, Theodore: *Winning of the West*, four volumes, G. F. Putnam & Sons, New York, 1869.

Rothrock, Mary U.: *Early Traders Among the Cherokee.* East Tennessee Historical Publication, 1934.

This Is Tennessee, Kingsport Press, Kingsport, Tennessee, 1963.

Royce, C.C.: *The Cherokee Nation of Indians.* A narrative of their official relations with the Colonial and Federal Governments. Fifth Annual Report, Bureau of Ethnology, 1883-1884, Government Printing Office, Washington, D.C., 1887.

Indian Land Cessions in the United States, Eighteenth Annual Report of the Bureau of American Ethnology, 1896-1897, Government Printing Office, Washington, D.C., 1899.

Sanders, W.L., Editor: Colonial Records of North Carolina (10 Volumes); State Records of North Carolina (20 Volumes), Raleigh, North Carolina.

South Carolina Records: Colonial and State Records (typed manuscript) *Indian Affairs*, Lawson McGee Library, Knoxville, Tennessee.

Starr, Emmett: *Early History of the Cherokee.* Embracing: aboriginal customs, religion, laws, folklore, and civilization. 1917.

History of the Cherokee Indians, and Their Legends and Folklore, The Warden Company, Oklahoma City, 1921.

(Starr's histories are important as tribal and genealogical sources.)

Timberlake, Henry: *Memoirs*, London, England, 1765. Reprint, annotated with index by Samuel Cole Williams, Watauga Press, Johnson City, Tennessee, 1927.

Tucker, Norma: *Nancy Ward, Ghighau of the Cherokee.* Georgia Historical Quarterly #21, 1962.

Weeks, Stephen B.: *General Joseph Martin and the Revolution in the West.* American Historical Association, Annual Report, 1895.

Williams, Samuel Cole: *Early Travels in the Tennessee Country, 1540-1800.* The Watauga Press, Johnson City, Tennessee, 1928. Reprint 1970 by Franklin Book Reprints, Nashville, Tennessee. Book includes records of explorers, traders, government agents, captives, and missionaries; also items from Adelaide Fries' records of the Moravians in North Carolina, and missionaries to the Cherokee. 3 volumes, North Carolina Historical Commission, Raleigh, North Carolina.

Dawn of Tennessee Valley and Tennessee History. The Watauga Press, Johnson City, Tennessee, 1937.

Tennessee During the American Revolutionary War. Tennessee Historical Commission, Nashville, Tennessee, 1944 (reprint 1975).

The Lost State of Franklin. The Watauga Press, Johnson City, Tennessee, 1924. Reprint by Franklin Book Reprints, Nashville, Tennessee, 1970.

Wright, Muriel H. *Springplace Moravian Mission — Cherokee Nation*, with genealogical notes of Miss Clara Ward and other sources. Also genealogy of Lowery family and Ward family. Co-operative Publishing Co., Guthrie, Oklahoma, 1940.

INDEX

Abingdon, Virginia 46
Adair, James 8, 73
Adair, Walter 81
Adams, John 76
Adawehi (Medicine Men) 13
Alabama 62, 76
Allen, Penelope 77
Amhearst, Jeffrey ..19, 20, 21, 25
Amovey District 83
Ancoowah 72
Ani-Ga-To-Ge-Wi
 (Wild Potato People) 5
Ani-Gi-Lo-Hi (Long Hair People) 5
Ani-Kawa (Deer People) 5
Ani-Sa-Ho-Ni (Blue People) 5
Ani-Tsi-S-Kwa (Bird People) 5
Ani-Waya (Wolf Clan) 5
Ani-Wodi (Paint People) 5
Ani-Yunwiya (Principal People) ..3
Appalachian Mountains ..7, 27, 56
Arcowee 82
Arkansas River 79
Armstrong, James 72
Atlantic Seaboard 4, 29
Attakullakulla 4, 9, 12, 13, 15,
 16, 18, 19, 20, 21, 24, 25, 27, 34,
 35, 36, 37, 38, 39, 52, 53, 54, 64,
 65, 66, 82, 83
Augusta, Georgia 59
Avery, Waightstill 54
Barker, Joseph 8
Bartram, William 76
Battle Creek 82
Battle of Horseshoe Bend 79
Battle of Island Flats 45
Battle of the Bluffs 63, 64
Bay's Mountain 55
Bean, John 34
Bean, William (Mrs.) ...47, 48, 53
Bean, William 33
Bell (Ensign) 16
Bell (Lieutenant) 19
Bench 70
Benge, Bob 73
Benton, Tennessee 82, 83
Big Bullet 54
Big Creek 57, 58
Big Pigeon River 67
Biles, Joseph 8
Black Drink 5
Black Fox 72, 73
Blackburn, Gideon 77
Bloody Fellow (Nooneteyah) ...37,
 70, 72
Blount, William .37, 72, 73, 74, 76
Blue Ridge Mountains 27, 50
Bold Hunter 72
Boone's Creek 33
Boone's Gap 33
Boone, Daniel 33, 35
Boyd Creek Battle 60
Boyd's Creek 60, 61
Brainerd, Tennessee 77
Branham, Jamie 34
Bristol, Tennessee-Virginia 33
Broad River 25
Brown, Jacob ..34, 35, 39, 46, 64

Brown, Ruth 35
Brown, Thomas 59
Buchanan, Alexander 63
Buchanan, John 63
Buffalo Creek 71
Bull (Governor) 20, 21, 24, 26
Burial Ceremony 73
Byrd (Colonel) 20
Byrd, Richard 25
Byrd, William 21
Calhoun (Secretary of War) 79
Calhoun, Georgia 77
Calhoun, Tennessee 79
Caloogee 61
Calvitt, Frederick 54
Cameron, Alexander ...34, 35, 48,
 49, 51, 52, 53, 54, 55, 56, 64
Campbell (Colonel) 59
Campbell (Governor) 40, 41
Campbell, Arthur 60, 61,
 62, 64, 70
Campbell, David 69
Canada 29, 57
Cane Creek 52
Cape Fear River 40
Carter's Valley 45, 46, 48
Carter, John 46
Cartoogechaye Creek 50
Caswell, Richard 41
Cates, M.O. 82
Cauquelehanah 72
Charles Town 8, 9, 13, 14,
 16, 17, 18, 19, 21, 24, 26
Charleston, South Carolina 40,
 41, 59
Charlotte, North Carolina 59
Chattahoochee River 49, 58
Chattanooga, Tennessee 54,
 57, 77, 82, 83
Cherokee Billy 35, 36
Cherokee Childhood 10
Cherokee Country - Map 22
Cherokee Government 3, 3
Cherokee Phoenix 77
Cherokee Syllabary 77
Chester County, Pennsylvania ..82
Chestowee 62, 76
Chestue 62
Chia-koneskie 72
Chickamauga 55, 59, 61,
 62, 66, 73, 74
Chickamauga Creek 54, 58
Chickamaugan Indians 57, 62,
 65, 69, 70, 71
Chickasaw Indians 42, 73
Chickasaw Killer 72
Chicken, George 13
Chilhowee 61
Chilhowie 70
Chimney Top Mountain 51
Chistowee 61
Chiswell Mine 27
Choctaw Indians 42, 73
Chota 3, 4, 7, 10, 13, 15, 16,
 18, 24, 25, 34, 36, 40, 42, 44, 47,
 48, 52, 53, 57, 59, 61, 62, 65, 66,
 69, 70, 72, 74, 75, 82, 83

Christian, William 50, 51, 52,
 53, 54, 64, 65
Chuleoah 72
Citico......................53
Clans....................3, 5
Clark, Elijah 61
Clark, George Rogers 57, 58
Cleveland, Benjamin 54
Cleveland, Tennessee 79
Clinch River 33, 50
Clinch Valley 48
Clinch Valley Settlement 54
Clinton (General) 40, 41, 59
Clogoittah 9
Clymer, George 76
Cocke, William 69
Columbus, Christopher 29
Communistic Republic 13
Conasauga River 71
Continental Congress 40, 64
Cooper, James 47
Cooper, Joseph 8
Coosa River 65
Coosawatee River 71, 77
Corkran, David H...........75
Cornstalk...................43
Cornwallis (General) 58, 59
Council House 28
Council of Safety 71
Cowee Creek 50
Coyatee 65, 69, 74
Coytmore, Richard 16, 19
Crabtree, William 35
Creek Indians ...5, 16, 42, 50, 52,
 57, 62, 66, 71, 73, 79
Creswell, William 46
Critington, Ally 80
Cross Creek 36, 41
Crows Creek 19
Cuba......................29
Cumberland Basin 62
Cumberland Gap 35, 58
Cumberland River 36, 40, 68
Cumberland Settlements 58,
 59, 69, 71, 73
Cuming, Alexander 9
Cummings, Charles 46
Dangerous Man 78
Dartmouth (Lord) 40
Dauge, James 8
Davidson River..............52
Davidson's Fort 50
Dearborn, Henry 78
Delaware Indians 4, 42
Demere (Captain) 20
Desoto 6
Devil's Fork Trail 71
Dewitt Corners, South Carolina .55
Dinwiddie (Governor) 15, 16
Donelson Line Survey 34
Donelson, John 58
Double Springs 51
Doublehead 70, 72, 73, 79
Dougherty, Cornelius 8
Dowie, David 8
Duck River 79
Dumplin Creek 67

Dungan's Mill 54
Dunsmore (Governor) 39
Early Cherokee Cultures 6
Eaton Station 45
Eaton's Fort 46
Eaton, J.H. 81
Echota 26, 77
Edisto River 9
Elizabethton, Tennessee 33, 37
English Traders 8
Estatoe 17
Etchoe 19, 20
Etchoe Pass 21
European Traders 7
Falling, William 36
Fauquier (Governor) 26
Fayetteville, North Carolina .36, 41
Federal Constitution 69
Federal-Cherokee Treaty 76
Ferguson, Patrick 59
Fields, Nancy 80
Fisk, Moses 35
Five Killer 48, 75, 81, 83
Flint Creek 71
Florida 29, 66
Forbes Camp 16
Fort Charlotte 40
Fort Chiswell 27
Fort Dobbs 15
Fort Lee 44, 45
Fort Loudoun 15, 16, 17, 19,
  20, 24, 25, 26, 37, 52
Fort Patrick Henry .50, 51, 54, 55
Fort Prince George 15, 16, 18,
  19, 20, 21, 24, 25, 49
Fort Robinson 25
Fort Watauga 54
Fort Williams 54
Foster (Lieutenant) 19
Four Mile Creek 83
Fox, Susanna 80
Franklin County, Georgia 75
Franklin, North Carolina .9, 21, 50
Franklin, State of ...67, 68, 69, 71
French Broad River ...50, 51, 52,
  53, 61, 67, 68, 69, 70, 72
French Lick 58, 62
French Traders 8
French-Indian War 15, 21
Friderici 77
Gage (General) 41
Gap Creek 47
Georgia ...3, 4, 5, 13, 27, 32, 33,
  40, 48, 53, 55, 62, 75, 78, 79, 81
Gill, Peter 63
Gillespie's Station 70
Gist, Nathaniel 52, 54
Glass 70
Glenn (Governor) 15
Goodale, Thomas 8
Grant (Lieutenant) 48
Grant, James 21, 24, 25
Grant, Ludovich 8
Greasy Cove 54, 71
Great Britain 10
Great Island Town 38, 52
Great Mortar 16, 19
Great Tellico 13, 15, 25, 75
Greene, Nathaniel 64

Greeneville, Tennessee 67, 68
Greer, Delbert 58
Gulf of Mexico 29, 78
Gunrod, Widow 80
Haines, Gregory 8
Hamilton, Henry 57
Hammond (Colonel) 49
Hampton (Lieutenant) 49
Hancock Hill 83
Hancock, M.H. 83
Hanging Maw 59, 69, 70, 72
Hard Labor Treaty of 1768 27
Harlan, Caty 80
Harlan, Elizabeth 77, 83
Harlan, Ellis 51, 52, 59, 60
Harlan, Nancy 82
Hart, Nathaniel 36
Hatton, William 8
Hawkins County, Tennessee 46
Heckewelder, John 69
Henderson, Richard 36, 37,
  38, 39, 40
Henry, Patrick..51, 52, 54, 56, 57
Hildebrand, Barbara 83
Hildebrand, Brice 83
Hildebrand, Catherine 83
Hildebrand, Delilah 83
Hildebrand, Elizabeth 82, 83
Hildebrand, Ellis Harlan 83
Hildebrand, George 77
Hildebrand, Isaac 83
Hildebrand, Jack 4, 83
Hildebrand, James 83
Hildebrand, Jennie 83
Hildebrand, John ...77, 81, 82, 83
Hildebrand, Joseph 83
Hildebrand, Lewis W. 83
Hildebrand, Margaret 83
Hildebrand, Mary 83
Hildebrand, Mary Elizabeth 83
Hildebrand, Michael 77, 83
Hildebrand, Minerva 83
Hildebrand, Nannie 83
Hildebrand, Peter 77, 82, 83
Hildebrand, Rachel 83
Hildebrand, Sarah 77
Hildebrand, Stephen 83
Hildebrand, Walker 83
Hiwassee 24, 61, 62
Hiwassee Garrison......... 77, 81
Hiwassee River 4, 50, 76,
  77, 82, 83
Holland 29
Holston River 33, 39, 46, 50,
  53, 54, 55, 56, 57, 64, 68, 72, 79
Holston Settlement 6, 44, 53,
  54, 62, 64
Holston Treaty 76, 82
Holston Valley 48
Hominy Creek 50
Hominy River 52
Hopewell Treaty 69, 70,
  71, 72, 79
Hopewell, South Carolina 67,
  68, 76
Hopper, Granny 27
Hot House 13
Householder, Susan 77
Hubbard (Major) 70

Huger, Isaac 41
Hunochatutloh................ 72
Ireland 26
Island Flats 47, 48, 49, 55
Jack, Jeremiah 65
Jack, Samuel 48, 49
Jackson, Andrew 79
James Island 41
Jarnigan, Lawyer 81
Jefferson, Thomas ..26, 56, 61, 78
Jenkinson, Daniel 8
Johnson, William 27, 70
Jonesborough, Tennessee 56
Junaluska 79
Justice, Richard 70, 73
Kai-a-tee 61
Kanuga 21
Kaskaskia 57
Kateh 72
Kealooske 72
Keleric (Governor) 16
Kennedy, George 63
Kennesaw 72
Kenoteta 72
Kentucky 35, 36, 37, 38,
  55, 58, 71, 73, 79
Kentucky River.............. 27
Keowee River 4, 15,
  16, 49, 67, 68
Keshu-kaunee 72
King Fisher 3, 4
King George II 9, 26
King George III 27
King's Mountain 59, 60
King's Mountain Battle 59
King, Duane H........... 58, 66
Kingfisher ..60, 62, 72, 75, 82, 83
Kingsport, Tennessee 44, 45,
  64, 75, 79
Kirk, John 70
Knox (General)............... 71
Knoxville, Tennessee ...70, 72, 77
Kollannah 9
Koolaqua 72
Lane (Lieutenant) 60
Lanier, Robert 54
Lantagnac 16
Leiper (Captain) 63
Lenni-Lennape 4
Lewis, Andrew 15, 25
Lick Creek 51
Lillington, Alexander 41
Limestone Creek 45
Limestone, Tennessee 44
Little Fellow 4, 62, 75
Little Mills River 52
Little Owl 52, 70, 73
Little River 53
Little Tennessee River ..4, 15, 17,
  50, 52, 53, 65, 69, 70, 72, 82
Little Turtle 73
Lochaber Treaty 27, 34
London, England 9, 12, 13
Long Fellow ...48, 52, 62, 75, 83
Long Hunter 33
Long Island ...25, 41, 45, 50, 53,
  54, 55, 56, 57, 60, 64, 65, 75, 79
Long Island Treaty 59
Long Island Treaty Meet ...56, 64

Long Will 72
Long, Alexander 8
Lookout Mountain 54, 57, 58
Lookout Mountain Town 73
Louisiana Purchase 78
Lower Towns 4, 9, 25, 41, 48, 49, 50, 53, 55, 65, 74
Lowery, George 81, 82
Lucas, Isaac 63
Lyttleton (Governor) 16, 17, 18, 20
Map - Cherokee Claims, 1785 .. 68
Map - Cherokee Country 31
Marion, Francis 21
Martin (Governor) 39, 40
Martin, John 81
Martin, Joseph 56, 57, 59, 60, 61, 62, 64, 65, 67, 70, 71, 72, 74, 75, 76, 83
Martin, Josiah 35
Martin, Nannie 77, 83
Martin, William 57, 74, 75
Maytoy 9
McCarter (General) 71
McCormack, John 25
McCormick 54
McCoy, A. 80
McDaniel, Catherine 27
McDonald, Donald 41
McDonald, John ... 54, 57, 58, 59
McDowell, John 35
McIntosh, Jenny 80, 81
McIntosh, John 81
McIntosh, Lachlan 67, 76
McLemore, Robert 72
McMinn, Joseph 79, 81, 82
Meigs, Jonathan 78, 79
Menefee, James 62, 63
Merewether, David 79
Middle Towns ... 4, 9, 21, 24, 25, 41, 48, 50, 51, 53, 56, 64
Middleton (Colonel) 21
Mieliqua 61
Miller, W.S. 81
Milligan College, Tennessee 71
Miln, Alexander 19
Mingo Indians 42
Missionary Ridge 77
Mississippi Basin 29
Mississippi River 32, 66, 67, 78, 80
Mississippi Valley 9, 15, 71
Mobile River 61
Mohawk Indians 42
Montgomery, Archibald 19, 20
Montgomery, John 57, 58
Moonshaw, Joseph 63
Moore's Creek Bridge 41
Moore, James 41
Moore, Samuel 47, 53
Morgan, M. 80
Morganton, North Carolina .35, 70
Moultrie, William 21, 41
Mount Pleasant 54
Mouse Creek 81
Moytoy 16
Mud Creek 52
Mulkey, Jonathan 46
Muscle Shoals 79
Muskogeans (Creeks) 3

Nan-ye-hi (Nancy Ward) 3
Nantahala Mountains 3, 50
Nantuca Indians 42
Nashborough 58, 62, 63
Nashville, Tennessee 58, 68
Neowee 21
Neowee Pass 49
Nequasse 20
Nequassee 9
New England 32
New Hampshire 27, 40
New Orleans 16, 66
New River 39
New World 29, 32
Newell's Station 71
Nicholson (Governor) 8, 78
Nolichucky River 34, 35, 39, 45, 46, 47, 53, 54, 56, 68
Nolichucky Settlement 6, 34, 44, 54, 60, 62, 64, 67
Nolichucky Valley 45
Nontuaka 72
North Carolina 4, 25, 32, 33, 34, 39, 48, 49, 52, 53, 54, 56, 64, 67, 68, 69, 70, 71, 72, 73, 75, 77, 78, 79, 81
Nottely River 4, 50
Ocoee River 75, 82, 83
Oconaluftee River 50
Oconaluftee Village 28
Oconee River 68
Oconostota 3, 4, 13, 15, 17, 18, 19, 20, 21, 34, 37, 39, 42, 52, 53, 54, 55, 59, 64, 65, 66
Ocuma 72
Ohio River 27, 72
Oklahoma 26, 73
Oklahoma Cherokee 4
Old Abram 37, 45, 46, 47, 70
Old Fields 33
Old Flats 44
Old Fort, North Carolina 50
Old Hop (Cherokee Emperor) 4
Old Natchez 77
Old Tassel 53, 55, 56, 59, 64, 67, 68, 69, 70, 72
Ole Caesar 24
Olinger, Danny E. 66
Onatoy 20
Oosenaleh 72
Oothcaloga, Georgia 77
Osage Indians 79
Osioota 43
Ostenaco ... 16, 18, 24, 25, 26, 35
Ottawa Indians 42
Oukah Ulah 9
Ounaconoa 9
Outlaw, Alexander 69
Overhill Country 4, 5, 6, 7
Overhill Towns 8, 9, 24, 25, 42, 47, 50, 51, 52, 53, 55, 56, 57, 59, 61, 62, 65, 66
Overmountain Men 59, 61, 62
Overmountain Settlements 42
Palmetto Log Fort 41
Paris Peace Treaty 66
Parker (Admiral) 41
Pensacola, Florida 41, 42, 53
Phillips, Edna Manley 75

Pickens, Andrew 67, 76
Pigeon River 50
Polk County, Tennessee 82
Powell Valley 48
Preston, William 54, 64
Priber, Christian 13
Price, Thomas 36
Prince Sealilosken 9
Proclamation Line of 1763 ....27, 28, 33, 34
Qualla Indians 4, 79
Quapaw Indians 79
Rankin, William 66
Reedy River 27
Revolutionary War 32, 33, 39, 66, 69, 78
Reynolds, Joshua 26
Richland Creek 50
Roan Creek 33
Roanoke River 53
Robertson, Charles 39
Robertson, James (Mrs.) 63
Robertson, James ..33, 34, 36, 46, 51, 54, 56, 57, 58, 62, 72
Rocky Fork 71
Rocky Mountains 78
Roddy, James 60
Rogers, Margaret Lavinia 26
Rogers, Will 26
Rogersville, Tennessee 54, 57
Roosevelt, Theodore 45, 49, 76
Ross, John 79, 80, 81
Russell, George 33
Russell, John 33
Russell, William 50
Rutherford, Griffith ..3, 48, 49, 50
Ryan, John 34
Sale Creek 58, 77
Salem, North Carolina 19
Salisbury District 50
Salisbury, North Carolina ... 15, 40
Saloue 17, 18, 25
Saluda River 9, 55
Santee River 9
Sappling Grove 33
Sattooga 61
Savannah River 55
Savannah, Georgia 59
Sawuteh 72
Schneider, Martin 7
Schweinitz 76, 82
Scittigo 61
Scott's Creek 50
Seagrove, James 71
Seneca 49
Sequoyah 77
Sequoyah, Mollie 28
Settico 16
Sevier County, Tennessee 60
Sevier, John ... 46, 51, 54, 58, 59, 60, 61, 62, 64, 67, 70, 71
Sevier, Valentine 54
Sevier, Valentine, Jr. 51
Sharpe, William 54
Shawnee Indians ...42, 50, 57, 73
Shelby, Evan ...33, 54, 57, 58, 64
Shelby, Isaac 33, 57, 59
Shelby, James 45
Sherrill, Catherine 46

Shorey, William 26
Skiuga 72
Soco Creek 50
South Carolina . . . 4, 8, 15, 17, 20,
  25, 27, 33, 48, 49, 50, 74, 75, 78
Southeastern Tribes 5
Southwest Territory 67, 71, 72
Spain 29, 66, 67
Spring Place, Georgia 77
Springstone, Henry William . 59, 60
St. Augustine, Florida 40
St. Claire (General) 73
St. Mary's River 76
Standing Turkey 19, 25
Starr, Caleb 51, 82
Steiner 76
Stekoa 50
Steniner 82
Stephen, Adam 25
Sticoy 50
Stuart, Henry . . . 34, 35, 40, 42, 44
Stuart, James 54
Stuart, John 20, 26, 27,
  40, 41, 42, 59
Sumpter, Thomas 25, 26
Surry County 50
Swan Pond 60
Swannanoa Gap 50
Swannanoa River 50, 52
Swanson, Edward 63
Sycamore Shoals 33, 35, 36,
  37, 40, 41, 59
Sycamore Shoals Treaty 73
Taliwa 44
Taliwa Battle 3
Talli-tahee 72
Taloteeskee 72
Tame Doe 4, 83
Tanasi Warrior 37
Tarlton, Banastre 59
Tarpin, Widow 80
Tasso 21
Tatham, William 46, 56
Tathtowe 9
Telasee 61
Telico 61
Tellico 9
Tellico Block House 74, 81, 82
Tellico River 4, 82
Tenasi 13
Tenasse River 61
Tennessee 4, 13, 33, 36,
  52, 67, 76, 78, 79
Tennessee River 54, 55, 68, 79
The Badger 52, 73
The Beaver 70
The Bench 73
The Canoe 73
The Glass 73
The Hanging Maw (Scolacutta) . 37

The Raven 24, 37, 39, 42,
  45, 46, 51, 52, 53, 54
The Tassel (Kaiyah-tahee) 37
Thomas, Isaac . . 20, 42, 44, 59, 60
Tiftoe 18
Tilthammer Rock 55
Tilthammer Shoals 55
Timberlake, Allison 26
Timberlake, Levi 26
Timberlake, Richard 25, 26
Timotlee 61
Tomotley 25, 52
Toqua 47, 52
Toque 53, 61
Trail of Tears 32
Transylvania Agreement 39
Transylvania Company 37
Treaty of Holston 72
Treaty of Tellico Blockhouse . . . 73
Tribal Towns 3
Tryon Mountain 27
Tsale-oono-yeh-ka 72
Tsistuna-gis-le (Wild Rose) 5
Tuckasee the Terrapin 37
Tuckasegee 58
Tuckasegee River 4, 50, 64
Tuckaseh 72
Tuckshalene 72
Tugaloo 13
Tugaloo River 4, 49, 55, 75
Tulluluh River 49
Turtle at Home 73
Tuskega-tahee 72
Tuskegee 47, 52, 53
Unicoi County, Tennessee . . 54, 71
United States 64, 67, 69, 71
United States Congress 32
Upper Settlement 3
Ustanali 71
Valley River 4, 50
Valley Settlements . . . 4, 9, 21, 41,
  48, 49, 50, 51, 53, 55, 56, 77
Vann, Joseph 39
Vincennes 57
Virginia 8, 15, 16, 20, 21,
  24, 25, 26, 27, 32, 33, 34, 39, 42,
  45, 46, 48, 53, 54, 56, 64, 70, 75
Wabash 73
Wachovia 36
Wafford Settlement 79
Walker, Asty 80
Walker, Elizabeth 80
Walton, Jesse 54
Ward, Betsy 4, 27, 57,
  64, 65, 75, 83
Ward, Brian 26
Ward, Bryant 4, 19, 26, 27,
  57, 74, 75, 82, 83
Ward, Catherine 4, 60, 83
Ward, Charles 27

Ward, George 27
Ward, James 27
Ward, John 26, 27, 60
Ward, Nancy Lucy 27
Ward, Samuel 27
Ward, Susie 27
Warrior Ford 50
Washington County, Tennessee . . 58
Washington, D.C. 79
Washington, George 15, 16,
  71, 72, 76
Watauga Association 35, 39
Watauga Fort 47
Watauga Purchase 39
Watauga River . . 33, 37, 39, 40, 48
Watauga Settlement 6, 34, 35,
  36, 42, 44, 46, 54, 57, 62, 64
Watauga Valley 33, 45
Watauga, Tennessee 54
Water Hunter 72
Watts, John 70, 72, 73, 74
Wauhatchie 17
Wava Gap 3
Wayah Gap 50
Wayne, Anthony 74
Waynesville, North Carolina 50
White's Fort 72
White, Zachariah 63
Whittier 50
Wiggam, Eleazar 8, 9
Wilderness Trail 58
Wilkes County, North Carolina . . . 54
Willenawah (Great Eagle) . . . 19, 37
William and Mary College 26
Williams, Jack 82
Williams, Joseph . . . 50, 53, 56, 64
Williams, S.G. 81
Williamsburg, Virginia 26
Williamson, Andrew 49, 50
Willinaw 25
Wilmington, North Carolina . . 40, 41
Wilson Hill 83
Wilson, Thomas 80
Winchester, Virginia 16
Winston, Joseph 50, 54
Winston-Salem,
  North Carolina 16, 36
Wolf Clan 10, 82
Wolf Hills 35, 46
Woman Holder, Widow 80
Womankiller Ford 82, 83
Woodland People 6
Yadkin River 16, 33, 53
Yadkin River Valley 19
Yellow Bird 72
Yona-watleh 72
Young Kitegisky 70
Young, Robert 54
Zionville 33